WORLD RELIGIONS SERIES
Series Editor: W. Owen Cole

Christianity

W. Owen Cole, B.A., B.D., M.Phil., Ph.D., Dip.Ed.

West Sussex Institute of Higher Education

Stanley Thornes (Publishers) Ltd

First published in 1989 by:
Stanley Thornes (Publishers) Ltd
Ellenborough House
Wellington Street
CHELTENHAM GL50 1YW

97 98 99 00 01 / 10 9 8 7 6 5

Typeset by Tech-Set, Gateshead, Tyne & Wear.
Printed and bound in Great Britain at T. J. International, Padstow.

British Library Cataloguing in Publication Data

Cole, W. Owen (William Owen) 1931–
  Christianity
  1. Christianity
  I. Title   II. Series
  200

ISBN 1–871402–08–5

Acknowledgements

Those who have helped me to write this book are too numerous for me to mention for they include past and present students, Christians in Britain, India, and Pakistan, and people of other faiths through whom my own perceptions of Christianity have been sharpened. More precisely, a considerable debt is owed to friends in the Shap Working Party on World Religions in Education, and to those in the Chichester Project, who have given so much thought to presenting Christianity as a world religion, especially John Rankin and Alan Brown, though my own journey began with comments made by a student in Leeds on returning from a teaching practice. Mavis Simpson confessed to teaching Islam in a way which children found exciting and interesting, but presenting her own religion, Christianity, in a dull and boring manner.

Specific gratitude must be expressed to Paul Baker, Bill Gray, Paul Lyons, Ruth Mantin, Isobella Maw, Fran Morley and Douglas Scrimgeour. Finally, as always, I owe the greatest expression of thanks to my wife, Gwynneth, for I could write nothing without her loving support.

W. Owen Cole

The author and publishers are grateful to the following for permission to reproduce material:

© Andes Press Agency, cover and pages 9, 35, 39, 49, 52, 55, 73, 81, 97, 109, 110, 116, 119 ● Bayerisches Nationalmuseum, page 5 ● Revd Clinton Bennett, page 102 ● British/Israel Public Affairs Centre, page 104 ● British Library, page 85 ● Trustees of the British Museum, cover and page 7 ● Catholic Building Society, page 93 ● Christmas Archives, pages 61, 66 ● Corinium Museum, Cirencester, page 47 ● Keith Ellis Collection, pages 37, 40, 44 ● English Heritage, page 21 ● Episcopal Diocese of Massachusetts, page 77 ● Sally and Richard Greenhill, page 72 ● The Mansell Collection, pages 1, 27 (top), 29, 57 ● Ben May, page 82 ● Methodist Home Mission Division, page 32 ● National Monuments Record for Wales, page 24 ● By courtesy of The News, Portsmouth, page 65 ● Novosti Press Agency, cover and pages 10, 27 (bottom) ● Religious Society of Friends, page 43 ● Scottish Tourist Board, page 23 ● Skelmersdale Ecumenical Centre, page 75 ● Spanish National Tourist Office, page 64 ● Taizé Community, Cluny, France, page 78 ● The United Society for the Propagation of the Gospel, cover and page 3.

The author provided the photographs on pages 68 and 70.

The biblical quotes used in this book are all from the New English Bible © 1970 by permission of Oxford and Cambridge University Presses.

Every effort has been made to contact copyright holders and we apologise if any have been overlooked.

Contents

Preface

This book has been written for use by students in schools in the UK, but it attempts to present Christianity as a religion which is to be found world-wide. For the last five centuries, Christianity has been very European in form, largely because the missionaries who took it to Africa, India, America, and elsewhere, were European. They had a natural pride in their culture, and identified it with Christianity. This can be seen most clearly in Christmas cards which show shepherds or wise men dressed in western clothes, travelling across a landscape which they could see in their own country, certainly not in Israel. Now there are more Christians outside Europe than within it. They practise Christianity while retaining their own cultures. They also share in the leadership of the churches and play an important part in bringing the denominations closer together.

All religions are diverse and complex when we get to know them well. No one book can provide every detail. It is hoped that this one is accurate and presents a sound overview of Christianity, but there is also a need for the schools to build up their own resources. Some bibles need to be available for consultation, perhaps not all of the same edition. Hymn books, missals, prayer books, and local church magazines might also be collected. Photographs of the interiors and outsides of churches in the neighbourhood would be useful too.

Religions are alive. They should be studied as far as possible through the people who practise them as well as through books. The purpose of this book is to present Christianity as a living, dynamic faith so that the reader may understand what it means to be a Christian in terms of belief and practice. It is not my intention to try to convert the non-Christian reader or to damage the faith of those who are Christians. However, my approach in this book is not shared by everyone. To avoid causing offence or embarrassment to visitors to the school, to parents and to anyone who may become involved in the projects mentioned in this book, it would be advisable to explain my intentions as author.

Finally, while it is assumed that the reader has already learned something about the Christian tradition I have tried to keep these assumptions to a minimum. Christianity is the most difficult religion to write about or teach in the UK simply because of the presupposition that everyone is a Christian in the making and has imbibed the faith with the mother's milk. This never has been true, and is certainly not the case today, even in rural West Sussex.

W. Owen Cole

Jesus

The four portraits of Jesus in this chapter, and which you can see in colour on the cover of this book, differ from each other so much that you might not think they were of the same person unless you had been told.

Which parts of the world do you think they come from? What kind of person do you think the artist thought Jesus to be? (Write down your views and check them against mine on page 11.)

No one really seems to know what Jesus looked like. The Christians who compiled the New Testament included no descriptions of his appearance. Yet this collection of Christian writings tells us almost all we know about Jesus and mentions him on almost every page.

The Shroud of Turin

Some Christians believe this to be the earliest portrait of Jesus. It is the outline of a man's face from a linen shroud. The story goes that this piece of cloth covered the body of Jesus in the garden tomb where he was laid after his death. One of his followers preserved it after Jesus rose from the dead (see page 10). Crusaders brought it to Europe. At last it was given to Turin Cathedral in Italy.

Some people doubt whether the outline on the shroud is the face of Jesus. They do not

think the shroud can be so old. Scientific tests seem to have proved them right, but not everyone accepts the evidence. There is nothing to prove that the shroud was wrapped round Jesus' body. It could have been used for someone else.

There is also the mystery of how the imprint of a face came to appear on the shroud. Those who believe the shroud *did* cover Jesus suggest that when he rose from the dead, an energy was released which affected the shroud rather like light on a film. They claim that this has also affected the carbon-14 test evidence.

Part of the Shroud of Turin, showing what is said to be the face of Jesus.

Why spend so much time discussing a piece of cloth? One reason is that the shroud of Turin keeps popping in and out of the news. People studying Christianity should be aware of it. Another reason is that it is controversial. At the very beginning of studying Christianity we may as well realise that it is controversial and always has been. Diversity is part of the nature of the religion. There have always been some believers who would like all Christians to believe the same thing and the result has been persecution: Christians with political power using it to harm those who disagreed with them, perhaps by taking away their jobs, even by having them killed. However, today many Christians accept diversity. It says in the Bible, 'When in former times God spoke to our forefathers, he spoke in fragmentary and varied fashion through the prophets' (Hebrews 1:1–2).

EARLY NON-CHRISTIAN WRITINGS ABOUT JESUS

There are a few other references to Jesus in ancient writings. One is from the Talmud, a Jewish book:

> On the eve of Passover they hanged [crucified] Yeshu of Nazareth, and the herald went before him for 40 days and saying 'Yeshu of Nazareth is going to be stoned because he has practised sorcery and led Israel astray. Let everyone knowing anything in his defence come and plead for him'. But nothing was found in his defence and he was hanged on the eve of the Passover.
>
> Quoted in C. Chapman, *The Case for Christianity* (Lion, 1981)

Notice the name of the man executed. It is not Jesus but Yeshu. Yeshu, Jeshua, Joshua, are the Hebrew names by which Jesus was known in his lifetime. In the Greek world which Christianity spread into, his name was changed to its Greek form of Jesus. It is just like someone called Peter moving to France where he would become Pierre. Think of it: Jesus was probably never called 'Jesus' during the whole of his life!

Another passage is by a Roman writer called Tacitus. Tacitus was the son-in-law of a Roman general called Agricola, who conquered part of northern Britain and, perhaps, Scotland. Tacitus tells us about such Britons as Boudicca and Caratacus. He also described the way in which the Roman Emperor, Nero, persecuted Christians in Rome. He used them as scapegoats, people to blame for a fire which destroyed much of the city. Rumour said he started it:

> [Nero] subjected to extreme tortures those whom the mob called Christians and hated because of their crimes. The founder of this movement, Christus, has been executed in the region of Tiberius by the procurator, Pontius Pilate. Repressed for a moment, the deadly superstition broke out again, not only throughout Judea, where the disease had originated, but also throughout Rome where, from everywhere, all things atrocious or shameful flow together and are practised. Accordingly, those admitting to being Christians were first seized, then, by their information, a huge multitude were convicted, not so much of arson as of hatred for the human race.
>
> Tacitus, *Annals*, XV, 44

Another writer Suetonius, in his *Life of Claudius*, says that someone called 'Chrestus' caused riots in Rome. As a result the Emperor Claudius expelled all the Jews who were living in the city. Probably this refers to arguments among Jews over the claim that Jesus was the Messiah, but clearly the author was not clear about this. He probably did not care. The event may have taken place a few years before the same emperor launched the invasion of Britain.

These few passages are all the information that non-Christians provided about Jesus in the time when he lived, or shortly afterwards. They are probably enough to satisfy historians that someone called Yeshu or Jesus of Nazareth actually lived.

? Discuss why the evidence is so scanty. Some suggestions are given on page 12 but no one knows for sure what the reasons are. Your ideas are as good as those of anyone else if they are carefully thought out.

Tacitus refers to someone called 'Christus'. You may already know that some people use the word Christ instead of Jesus. Some use both and say Jesus Christ – so that one little boy once said Jesus' parents were Mr and Mrs Christ! Christ, however, is a title meaning anointed and refers to the claim that Jesus was the anointed one, the Messiah, whom Jews were hoping for and still expect. Christ is the Greek equivalent of Messiah just as Jesus is the Greek form of Yeshu.

CHRISTIAN WRITINGS ABOUT JESUS

The Christian writings about Jesus are published in one book called the New Testament. It is the main source of knowledge about Jesus, but even this provides only limited information about Jesus' life. There are four books called Gospels in the New Testament, Matthew, Mark, Luke and John, but only Matthew and Luke mention Jesus' infancy.

The Gospel According to St Matthew describes Jesus' birth – the visit of some 'wise men from the east', and an attempt by Herod, the ruler of Judaea, to track down the baby and kill him. To escape, Mary and Joseph took him to Egypt.

The Gospel According to St Luke links Jesus with someone called John the Baptist. It also contains stories of Jesus' parents travelling from Nazareth to Bethlehem where Jesus was born. In Bethlehem, Jesus was born in a stable, or more probably a cave, where shepherds found him and brought him gifts.

Luke's Gospel also provides the only information we have about Jesus' life from babyhood until he was about 30 years old. Luke says, 'Now it was the practice of his parents to go to Jerusalem every year for the Passover festival; and when he was twelve, they made the pilgrimage as usual' (Luke 2:41–3). Luke tells the story of Jesus' disappearance and his parents' eventual discovery of him debating with scholars of the Jewish scriptures in the Temple.

All four Gospels describe the last week of Jesus' life and his death, and the stories about his resurrection in great detail. More is known about the death and resurrection of Jesus than about the rest of his life, for reasons that we shall eventually discover. Jesus died in Jerusalem at the Passover festival of the Jews which he, as a Jew, was celebrating. He was crucified but, although he was definitely dead, his friends experienced him alive again some three days later.

?   Find out some details of Jesus' life for yourself. They can be read in many New Testament passages, especially Matthew 26–8, Mark 14–16, Luke 22–4 and John 18–21.

One reason why the New Testament tells us so little about Jesus' everyday life, his pastimes, how he got on with his family and so on, is because these things did not interest his followers. Christians believe that Jesus was someone who stood in a special relationship to God. They claim that he is unique, no one else has known God so fully, or been so close to him. They often call Jesus the Son of God as a way of expressing this special relationship. The teachings of Jesus will be looked at more fully in Chapters 12 and 13. However, some mention of them is needed here if we are to understand the New Testament stories about his life. Almost every story has a *meaning*. It is this meaning that matters most to Christians when they read them. Let us look at a few examples.

Birth Stories

After his birth astrologers from the east arrived in Jerusalem, asking, 'Where is the child who is born to be king of the Jews? We observed the rising of his star, and we have come to pay him homage' (Matthew 2:1–2). Understandably, but mistakenly, they went to the king in Jerusalem, before being redirected to Bethlehem by Jewish priests and religious teachers.

A nativity scene from Ethiopia.

Matthew does not tell us how many wise men or astrologers came or where they came from – China, India, or Persia. The message of the story is that Jewish scholars told the wise men that the Messiah would be born in Bethlehem (Matthew 2:6) but that the first people to worship him were non-Jews. The time came, about 20 years after the life of Jesus, when his followers, who were all Jews, argued about whether Gentiles, as they called the non-Jews, could become Christians. After all, Jesus had spent all his time preaching to Jews. Perhaps Matthew is using the story of the wise men to say that anyone who is guided by God may worship Jesus.

No one knows whether Luke knew the story of the wise men or not. He chooses to tell the birth of Jesus in a stable but his visitors are shepherds.

1 Discuss what kind of people would be attracted and encouraged by the story which Luke tells (Luke 2:4–20).
2 Read the birth and infancy accounts of Matthew and Luke and list the main headings of each in separate columns.
3 Are there any similarities at all between Matthew's and Luke's birth stories?

Many pages of the Gospels are taken up with the stories that Jesus told and the things that he did. These, together with his death, are ways of *teaching*, as we shall see.

The Family of Jesus Puzzle

'Is not this the carpenter, the son of Mary, the brother of James and Joseph and Judas and Simon? And are not his sisters here with us?'

Mark 6:3

Is there someone missing from this list? A name we would expect to find? Many of us would have begun with dad and then mum.

 Discuss why is there no mention of Joseph. There could be at least three answers. Can you think of them? (Check your suggestions against those on page 12.)

It must be admitted that some early manuscripts read, 'Is not this the carpenter's son?' So another answer could be that Mark *did* mention Jesus' father. If so, we still have to ask why many of the early copies of Mark do not refer to Jesus' father.

The birth stories recorded by Matthew (1:18–25) and Luke (1:26–38) say as clearly as possible that Mary was a virgin when she conceived Jesus. Matthew 1:25 may imply that Mary and Joseph enjoyed a normal married life after Jesus was born. The children mentioned in Mark 6:3 would be the result.

There have always been Christians eager to maintain the purity of Mary, people who believe that celibacy, life-long virginity, is preferable to marriage. The Roman Catholic church teaches that Mary was a virgin when she conceived Jesus, as the Bible says, but also that she remained a virgin. In 1854 it proclaimed the doctrine that Mary, alone among human beings was conceived immaculate and free from the stain of original sin. This was proclaimed as infallibly correct.

 If this teaching is accepted, how can Mark 6:3 be understood?

Most Christians accept Matthew 1:25 at its face value. Jesus was conceived in the way described by Matthew and Luke but grew up with younger brothers and sisters whose real parents were Mary and Joseph.

A minority of Christians regard the virginal conception as a legend which quickly grew up in Christian circles. They see no reason for thinking that Jesus should have been conceived and born differently to other people.

 Discuss what you think the story of the virginal conception of Jesus means.

Teachings

The most famous collection of Jesus' teachings is found in Matthew 5–7. It begins with the words, 'When he saw the crowds he went up the hill. There he took his seat, and when his disciples had gathered around him he began to address them. And this is the teaching he gave' (Matthew 5:1–2).

Today Christians call these chapters the Sermon on the Mount. They find it a helpful guide to many aspects of being a Christian. It has verses of encouragement when things are hard. It tells them how to live and how to treat other people. It includes the famous prayer which Jesus taught his disciples and which probably each Christian says every day, known as the Lord's Prayer.

However, the Sermon on the Mount has another meaning. Some 1400 years before Jesus, when his Jewish ancestors were escaping from Egypt, their leader Moses gathered them together at a mountain called Sinai. The story in the Bible, Exodus 20, says that he returned with two large stones. These had ten commandments written on them. The Hebrew people promised to obey these ten rules for living. In Matthew's Gospel Jesus climbs a hill too. He often refers to the ten commandments but adds some teaching of his own. For example, 'Do not commit murder' was one of the commandments. Jesus added, 'Do not nurse anger against anyone.' Such smouldering hatred is as bad as murder. It looks for ways of harming the person we hate and kills the spirit of love inside us. Was Jesus claiming to be greater than Moses?

The parables of Jesus

Often Jesus told stories when people asked him questions, or when he was teaching. He usually did this to make people think. The New Testament writers call these stories parables. They tend to be about everyday events but their meaning is related to Christian living.

One famous example is the Parable of the Prodigal Son. Read about it in Luke 15:11–32 and consider what it might mean. It could have many meanings depending on who is listening to the story. No answer is completely right or wrong. Religious studies is not like mathematics.

Now answer the following questions.

1 If you have thought of a meaning while reading the Parable of the Prodigal Son, write it down.
2 Jesus' audience was totally Jewish. What meaning might it have had for them?

3 Within 30 years of Jesus' ministry, many Christian communities would be mixed Jewish and Gentile. How might such a group understand the parable?

4 What might the parents of a runaway teenager make of the story today?

In answering each question, it might help you if you ask who the father, elder son and younger son are in each case. Now read the comments on page 12.

5 Read the Parable of the Workers in the Vineyard in Matthew 20:1-16. If you have an idea of what it might mean, write it down.

6 Imagine you are a Jew who did not keep the Sabbath, the fixed laws or other commandments, very carefully. What might the message of this parable be for you?

7 If you were a Gentile hearing this parable, might it give you any hope? Why?

Now look at the comments on page 12.

8 Write a few sentences explaining what a parable is.

Understanding the parables of Jesus   It always helps to try to discover the kind of situation in which Jesus told them. This may be difficult because by the time the New Testament writers put them into the Gospels, the Christian communities were either mixed Jewish and Gentile or even purely Gentile. The original meaning might be very difficult to trace.

We must always remember, however, that Christians feel that the parables are alive, they have a meaning for today. They are not just stories of long ago.

The miracles of Jesus

These are the most difficult form of Jesus' teaching to understand. With the miracles he taught in actions, not words. Often people argue about whether Jesus actually did turn water into wine or raised someone to life after he was dead, rather than trying to discover what the stories *mean*.

?

Let us look at two or three examples. First, the turning of water into wine at a wedding which Jesus attended. Read the story for yourself in John 2:1-10, and discuss what you think it means.

The account of the wedding at Cana is often read at weddings to remind the bride and groom that Jesus was once a wedding guest and approved of marriage. Sometimes his rather rude treatment of his mother attracts attention. However, the wedding feast was also a well-known Jewish symbol for the age of joy and deliverance which God would provide. This story, along with others in John's Gospel, says that the Jewish religion is dead and tasteless like the water in the jars, but that Jesus gives it life when he turns it into sparkling wine. Not all New Testament writers share this view of Judaism but it is a strong theme in John's Gospel.

Another well-known miracle story is one which tells of Jesus visiting Capernaum, the village of his friend Peter. There were crowds of people inside the house and at the door. A group of men brought a paralysed friend on his mattress hoping Jesus would cure him. They could not get past the throng so they took their friend on to the flat roof. From there they lowered him into the room where Jesus was. (Some houses may have had a kind of trap door – or did they actually make a hole in the thin plaster and wood roof?) Jesus said to the man, 'Your sins are forgiven,' then he told the man to get up and carry his mattress away with him, which the man did. The healing does not seem to have surprised anyone. Apparently these things were fairly common events in Jesus' time. However, by saying 'Your sins are forgiven' Jesus nearly caused a riot. 'Only God can forgive sins,' argued some of the people who were there. Christians believe that God gave Jesus this power.

The healing of the paralysed man shows how Jesus taught through his actions. This time the message was that God forgives sins. The Gospel writer – this time it is Mark – also uses the story to tell the reader that Jesus' ministry was controversial right from the start. Read the story for yourself in Mark 2:1–12. If you read the whole chapter and continue to chapter 3, verse 6, you will see that already some were plotting to be rid of Jesus.

?   Read Mark 2:1–28 and 3:1–6. Why do you think Jesus made enemies? (Turn to page 12 and check your ideas against those given there.)

This is not the place to discuss whether miracles actually happen or not. It is only important for our purpose to remember that we must not concentrate on arguing about the event. We must look for the *message*. Christians have never claimed that Jesus was the only person who did these things. Read Luke 11:14–20, where you will see that the dispute is about where the power of Jesus, and others who also cast out demons or healed the sick, came from.

Look up 'miracle' in several dictionaries and write down the best definition you can find. Discuss whether this definition is suitable for Jesus' miracles.

The Death and Resurrection of Jesus

Read Matthew 26:17–28:20, Mark 14:12–16:20 or Luke 22:7–24:53 before you go any further.

Jesus' death and resurrection concerned the New Testament writers more than anything else. Each of the four Gospels devotes about a quarter or third of the space to it. Because Jesus was crucified like any other common criminal, viewed by the authorities as a threat to the stability of Judaism or the Roman occupation, his followers had to 'put the record straight'.

All the Gospels agree that the trial was a rushed job. Arrested late at night, Jesus was dead by mid-afternoon on the next day. They also say that the charges were false, that the Roman Governor, Pontius Pilate, would have liked to set Jesus free and that Jesus was really the innocent victim of a plot.

The followers of Jesus also claimed that Jesus' death was God's will. Just before his arrest, Jesus prayed in the Garden of Gethsemane, 'Father, if it be thy will, take this cup away from me. Yet not my will but thine be done' (Luke 22:42). The Gospels suggest that Jesus had tried to prepare his followers for his death and resurrection for some time but without success. They could not believe that this man, who was the anointed Son of God, could end up suffocating to death slowly, crucified as a criminal – and at Passover time, too, when all Jews remembered and celebrated the deliverance of their ancestors from Egypt!

Jesus' death and resurrection are central to Christian belief. Christians believe that Jesus died on behalf of others. Sometimes they use the language of sacrifice. In John's Gospel a man called John the Baptist, Jesus' cousin, calls him 'The Lamb of God; it is he who takes away the sin of the world' (John 1:29). The same idea is present in one of the most famous verses of the Bible, 'God loved the world so much that he gave his only Son, that everyone who has faith in him may not die but have eternal life' (John 3:16). Jesus used the idea of paying a ransom to free someone in Mark 10:45, 'For even the Son of Man did not come to be served but to serve, and to surrender his life as a ransom for many.' On another occasion he said, 'There is no greater love than this, that a man should lay down his life for his friends' (John 15:13). He told them that they were his friends, and that they should love and serve one another as he had loved and served them. At the last meal which Jesus ate with his friends before his arrest, he took a bowl of water and a towel and washed the feet of his disciples, just as a slave would do (John 13:3–15). This was another way of making the same point.

Sometimes Christians have tried to be too precise in explaining how Jesus' death could deliver other people. Pushed too far, the idea of sacrifice can suggest a cruel God. What Christians insist on is that Jesus' death demonstrates the love of God, the promise of forgiveness of sins and the gift of eternal life.

It is very important for Christians to believe that Jesus died on behalf of others. It is even more important to believe that God raised him from the dead. If his grief-stricken friends, bewildered and full of despair at his death, had not become convinced that Jesus, the same Jesus who was their friend, had been brought back to life, they would have given up hope. There would be no Christianity.

1   Read some of the hymns which Christians sing on Good Friday about the meaning of the crucifixion of Jesus. List them under headings of Love, Sacrifice, Forgiveness and Other reasons.

2   Write a brief entry for *Who's Who* about Jesus, mentioning his parents, place of birth and the important incidents in his life which merit his inclusion in *Who's Who*.

3   Draw an outline map of the Mediterranean and Middle East. Mark on it the places mentioned in this chapter. Write notes on their importance in the story of Christianity. You can add more places to the map as you read this book.

4   Draw your own picture of Jesus, or write a description of the sort of man you think he was. When you have finished reading this book, look at your picture/description again. Have your ideas of Jesus changed? Why?

Throughout this chapter you have been asked to consider various questions and compare your views with my suggestions, which are set out below.

Page 1   What kind of person do you think the artists thought Jesus to be?
The Indian picture (page 3) seems to show a very spiritual man – pure, beyond the cares of the world. The Roman mosaic (page 7) is of a kind of father-figure. The Ethiopian picture (page 9) shows a much-protected child. The descent from the cross in the Russian icon (page 10) is of a man who really suffered. All the artists imagine a Jesus of their own culture. They are not interested in portraying a Palestinian Jew but in symbolism – Jesus if for everyone.

Page 3   Why is the evidence about Jesus in early non-Christian writings so scanty?
1   Historians in the ancient world, and very often today still, were interested in political figures and events connected with them. So it was Pontius Pilate and troubles in Rome which they recorded. They just happened to involve 'Christus'. Great people like Buddha, Muhammad and Guru Nanak were neglected in the same way. (How much attention does religion receive in books

on the twentieth century in the school library? If Mother Theresa, Martin Luther King or Mahatma Gandhi are mentioned, is it for religious or political reasons?)

2   The arguments and discussions which Jewish religious teachers had with one another were not written down at this time. Their disciples memorised them. Later, when the teachings of the rabbis were recorded, Christianity was no longer a movement within Judaism so naturally there would be no references to the new religion.

3   The Jesus movement did not seem very important at the time. It is not unusual for little material to exist about people in the past before the days of cheap newspapers, films and TV. For example, there are many things about Shakespeare which scholars have not been able to discover.

Page 6   Why is there no mention of Joseph in Mark 6:3?
There are three possible answers:
1   Joseph had already died when the words were written.
2   Joseph was only Jesus' adopted father.
3   Mark felt it might cause confusion if he said Jesus was the son of Joseph as well as the son of God.

Page 7   Possible meanings of the Parable of the Prodigal Son.
1   For Jews listening to Jesus it might have challenged any of them who believed that God was only interested in the godly who kept the Torah perfectly. Jesus' great appeal was to those who were not very observant.

2   Mixed congregations of Jews and Gentiles might have thought it referred to Jews, who like the older brother, had always been faithful to God. They might have been jealous that the newcomers, the Gentiles, seemed to be as precious to God as they were. Did not their worship of the One God from the time of Abraham count for anything?

3   John or Tracey, runaways in London, might not find a religious meaning at all. It might simply help them to make up their minds to go back home. On the other hand, their parents might feel like the father in the story.

Page 8   Possible meanings of the Parable of the Workers in the Vineyard.
1   A Jew who did not observe the instructions of the Torah very carefully might think that the parable was about him/her being given the chance of a new start and the promise of spiritual rewards based on sincerity not length of piety.

2   Gentiles might think that there was hope for them at this eleventh hour even though they lacked the 1500 years obedience to the covenant which Jews could be proud of.

Page 9   Why do you think Jesus made enemies?
Some reasons might be:
Jealousy   Jesus was a popular person; that always angers some people.
Fear   If Jesus and his followers caused trouble, the Roman authorities might make life even more difficult for their Jewish subjects.
Anger   Jesus criticised the Temple officials publicly. This threatened their livelihood and their power (Mark 11: 15–19).
Disappointment   Perhaps such a troublesome, popular man would lead a revolt against the Romans. He did not. Instead he even encouraged Jews to pay their taxes to their oppressors (Mark 12: 13–17)!

Chapter 2

The Beginnings of the Christian Church

DISCIPLES

When Jesus began his preaching ministry, he chose twelve of those who followed him, all Jews like himself, to be a close band of companions. He did this for at least two reasons:

- so that they could share his work – thirteen pairs of feet could cover more ground than one
- so that they could continue his ministry after he had left them.

In the Gospels we read of him sending them out two by two, sometimes to prepare a village for his coming, sometimes to do the kinds of thing that he did, pass on his teachings and heal the sick.

?

Why do you think Jesus sent them in pairs?

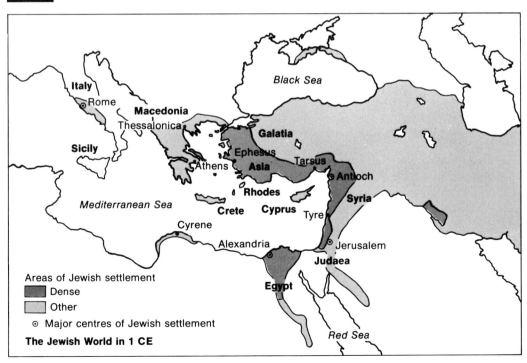

Areas of Jewish settlement

■ Dense

□ Other

⊙ Major centres of Jewish settlement

The Jewish World in 1 CE

There were no women in this band of special companions. This may well have been because of the risks involved. It was not safe for women to travel alone. A mixed group of men and women, often sleeping rough, would have provoked gossip. Jesus was a controversial enough teacher without giving people reason to spread rumours of sex scandals. Eastern societies have always been strict about such matters. Even today men and women rarely mix socially outside family gatherings.

The twelve constant companions are known as the *disciples*, a word meaning learner. Mark gives their names as Simon known as Peter, James and John (Zebedee's sons), Andrew, Philip, Bartholomew, Matthew, Thomas, James (the son of Alphaeus), Thaddaeus, Simon the Zealot, and Judas Iscariot (Mark 3:16, see also Luke 6:14).

There may have been a few reasons for Jesus choosing twelve disciples. It is a good size for a group – not too many, not too small. However, the number has often been regarded as symbolic. There were twelve tribes in ancient Israel. In the new age that Jesus was expected to introduce one disciple would lead each tribe. Clearly Jesus had far more than twelve followers, women among them, but the disciples were to be leaders of the new movement.

When the disciples' loyalty was put to the test for the first time, they proved unreliable. When Jesus was arrested they all deserted him. His enemies found it easy to capture him because one of the disciples, Judas Iscariot, told them where he could be found and led them to him. Simon Peter, who had always boasted about his bravery and loyalty, summoned up enough courage to follow Jesus to the palace of the High Priest, where he was being tried, but when a maidservant accused him of being one of Jesus' friends he said he did not know him.

From this unlikely collection of men the Christian community began. During the six weeks after the death of Jesus, the disciples rallied, so much so that at the festival of Pentecost, the next great Jewish celebration after Passover, Peter and the rest preached publicly that the Jesus who had been executed was the promised Messiah. These are some of the words which Peter spoke:

> 'Men of Israel, listen to me: I speak of Jesus of Nazareth, a man singled out by God and made known to you through miracles, portents, and signs, which God worked among you through him, as you well know. When he had been given up to you, by the deliberate will and plan of God, you used heathen men to crucify and kill him. But God raised him to life again, setting him free from the pangs of death, because it could not be that death should keep him in its grip.'
>
> Acts 2:22–4

These were strong, brave words from the man who had denied knowing Jesus. What had happened to bring about the change? Why had despair and cowardice been replaced by courage? There are three reasons:

- The disciples were sure that God had raised Jesus from the dead – after his death, they had met him in Jerusalem, by the Sea of Galilee and elsewhere.
- Jesus had shown understanding – he had not shouted at them for being disloyal but had forgiven Peter and almost acted as though they had done nothing wrong; his death was part of God's plan for demonstrating his love of humankind and forgiveness of their sins.
- Most importantly, Jesus had promised his disciples the Holy Spirit, his presence in a new way, within them wherever they were. They seemed to possess the power which they had seen in Jesus and this inspired them.

Discuss the view that some Christians have that Judas, the disciple who betrayed Jesus, was a saint because he was really helping God's will to be done! Most do not share this view.

APOSTLES

The companions were no longer disciples but *apostles*. Their task was to tell people about the ministry of Jesus, which they had experienced from beginning to end, and to be witness to the resurrection of Jesus, which they had seen. Apostle means sent. They were *sent* to do this job. The place of Judas was taken by a man called Matthias.

No one can prove that Jesus rose from the dead or that he had a special, unique relationship to God, that of son to father, but an important reason for Christians believing these things is the changed lives of the disciples. Another reason is that the promise of the Holy Spirit is one which many Christians since the time of the apostles, right up to today, have experienced.

Most of what is known about the early Christian community is contained in a New Testament book called the Acts of the Apostles. This was written by Luke, the writer of one of the Gospels. It is not really a history of the Church (the name Christians used to describe the community of those who believe in Jesus as their Lord and Saviour). It misses out some interesting things such as how Christianity reached Rome and how Simon Peter, and another famous Christian called Paul, died. Probably there was no need to mention them. The people for whom Acts was written are likely to have known these facts.

What they seem to have needed was information about Peter and Paul's lives before they went to Rome and especially anything that would help them to answer critics who said that Peter and Paul were a couple of troublesome criminals who deserved to be executed. The Roman Christians, for whom Luke's Gospel and the Acts of the Apostles were both probably written, could not have had an easy time arguing that one executed criminal, Jesus, was the Son of God, and that two of his followers, executed as criminals, were also innocent.

The picture that Acts gives of the first Christians is that they remained good Jews, worshipping in the Temple at Jerusalem every day. However, they differed from their fellow Jews by claiming that Jesus was the Messiah and, more than that, a person who was both human and divine. This created opposition. One Christian named Stephen was stoned to death and so became the first Christian martyr (Acts 7:54–8:1). (A martyr is someone who dies for her or his faith.) The Christians also met every day 'to break bread' (Acts 2:42). This phrase probably refers to a religious meal based on the last supper Jesus had with his disciples. They probably remembered his words and believed that he was with them in some special way.

One man who had been present at the stoning of Stephen was a Jew named Saul. He had no time for Christians and was employed by the Temple authorities to hunt down and arrest them. His job took him to the neighbouring province of Syria. As he was about to enter one of its chief cities, Damascus, something terrifying happened to him. He saw a blinding light and heard a voice which identified itself as Jesus. (The Jewish tradition has many accounts of God speaking through visions and dreams.) Blind and bewildered he was led into the city by his companions. The Christians in Damascus had had a no less disturbing experience. One of them, Ananias, had also had a vision. A voice had told him to go to the house where Saul was staying. This was something Ananias did not really want to do because he knew of Saul's reputation as a persecutor of the followers of Jesus. However, he obeyed the vision and restored Saul's sight. The outcome of the story is that Saul became a Christian. (The story of Saul's conversion is in Acts 9.) In most of the New Testament he is called by the Gentile version of his name, Paul, just as Jesus is.

CHRISTIANS AND NON-JEWS

One of the biggest debates among the first Christians concerned non-Jews. Could they become Christians or not? Some Christians said 'no', perhaps thinking that if Jesus had wanted Gentiles, as non-Jews were called, to become Christians he would have preached to them himself. Others were willing to admit them if they converted to Judaism first. Another group felt that everyone should be allowed into the Church so long as they shared its beliefs about Jesus. The argument lasted for some time. Paul was for admitting Gentiles. Peter kept changing his mind. Eventually Peter was won over. This is how it happened.

Peter was visiting Christians in the port of Joppa. One day, at about noon, he climbed the steps to the flat roof of the house where he was staying to pray. He felt hungry, and while he was waiting for a meal to be prepared he fell into a trance. He saw a great sheet the size of a ship's sail covered with food coming down from the sky. All kinds of food were on it including meats which Jews would not eat – things like crab, shellfish and, of course, pork. A voice said 'Up, Peter, kill and eat.' Horrified Peter refused. He had never eaten forbidden food in his life. Three times the sheet was lowered, Peter was told to 'kill and eat', and refused, and the voice also said, 'It is not for you to call unclean what God counts clean.'

Peter tried to puzzle out what the vision meant. Peter would not feel that hunger or the hot sun were adequate explanations. As he was thinking, someone came to Peter to tell him he had visitors. He went downstairs to find that messengers had come from a Roman army officer, a centurion called Cornelius. They wanted Peter to go with them to the house of Cornelius. It seemed the centurion had received a message from God to send for Peter. The messengers said he was a God-fearer, that is someone who respected Jewish religious teachings and attended the synagogue in Caesarea where he was stationed. But he was a Gentile. Peter might have hesitated to go. He might even have refused but for the vision. With some other Christians from Joppa he set out for Caesarea.

Cornelius was waiting for Peter, with his family and close friends. He told Peter that he had been told in a dream where Peter was staying and instructed to send messengers to ask him to come to Caesarea. Peter began to tell the gathering about Jesus' ministry, crucifixion and resurrection. They were filled with joy and ecstasy. Peter realised that the Holy Spirit which inspired him had also entered them. 'Is anyone prepared to withhold the water for baptism from these persons, who have received the Holy Spirit just as we did ourselves?' he asked. The Gentile Cornelius, his wife, family and friends were accepted into the Christian community by the rite of baptism. Peter had been won over. (The whole story can be found in Acts 10 and 11.)

When Stephen had been killed (see page 16), many Christians had left Jerusalem. They took their faith with them. They preached only to Jews, but in places like the great Syrian sea port of Antioch, Jews and Gentiles mixed easily. Some Gentiles were God-fearers like Cornelius. They became followers of Jesus. Paul and his friend Barnabas were sent to Antioch to see what was happening. They reported that it was true, Gentiles were becoming sincere believers. There was more evidence that Christanity was for everyone regardless of race or religion.

Incidentally it is only now that we should begin using the word Christian. Followers of the way of Jesus, or more usually Nazarenes, followers of Jesus of Nazareth, is the name that should be used until this point. Now, for the first time, in Antioch, the name Christian was used – to describe those people who believed that Jesus was God's anointed, the Messiah. The Greek for messiah is Christ (Acts 11:26).

The First Christian Council at Jerusalem

The Gentile issue had to be cleared up. By now there seemed little doubt that Gentiles might become Christians. They could already become Jews. Conversion was not the problem, but the process of becoming a Christian was. Some Jewish Christians argued that the way must be through conversion to Judaism first.

1 What reasons could you put forward in favour of the view that Gentiles should become Jews before becoming Christians?
2 What reasons could you give for opposing this view?

A meeting (council) was held to discuss this matter. You can read about the debate for yourself in Acts 15.

The decision of the gathering was that faith in Jesus was the only requirement for conversion to Christianity, and the keeping of four rules:

1 They should not eat food which had been offered for sacrifice in Greek or Roman or other temples. This meat was popular because it was often cheap. Only certain parts of an animal could be sacrificed and the rest was sold in the market: kidneys, liver, heart, such parts of an animal the rich would not eat and were not offered to the gods.
2 Sexual relations outside marriage were forbidden.
3 Animals or birds which had been strangled should not be eaten because they would still have blood in them. Jewish food laws required the blood to be drained away.
4 Blood should not be taken in any form. It might be in meat which had been strangled but also in whatever people ate in the ancient world which was like black pudding or gravy.

What reasons can you suggest for making the first rule?

The second rule was essential in a society where sexual morality was not considered important. Jews stressed loyalty in marriage, many Gentiles did not. It was also known that Christians talked about 'loving your neighbour'. Some people enjoyed inventing and passing on rumours that Christians indulged in love feasts which were really orgies.

Although Peter (sometimes called Simon) spoke and so did Paul and Barnabas, the chairperson who gave the final decision was a man called James. He was not an apostle. Elsewhere he is known as 'James, the Lord's brother', that is the brother of Jesus. According to legend he only came to believe that Jesus was God's anointed after the resurrection.

Can you think why James rather than Peter or another apostle might have become leader of the church in Jerusalem? (It may help you to answer this if you look up what the job of an apostle was.)

SPREADING THE WORD

In the year 66 CE many Jews revolted against their Roman overlords. Most Jewish Christians had already left Judaea and Galilee. Now the remainder went to such places as Egypt, Antioch, Rome, perhaps even to Persia which was outside the Roman Empire. They did not share the nationalistic views of the fellow Jews who, anyway, had sometimes persecuted them for their views about Jesus. Christianity almost disappeared from its homeland, though probably never totally. The main Christian cities were now Alexandria, Antioch and Rome, though there were also Christians in Spain and India by that time (the tomb of the apostle Thomas can be seen in Madras). The Jewish roots of the young religion were being forgotten.

By 79 CE it is possible that the Lord's Prayer (the prayer given by Jesus to his disciples) was already known in its Latin version, the language spoken in Italy. It begins with the words *Pater Noster*. By rearranging the letters, can you find them in this word puzzle (acrostic) below? It was first found on wall plaster from a Roman excavation in Cirencester, Gloucestershire in 1868. Two more were later found in Pompei (in 1925 and 1936) on pieces of wall plaster buried in the ashes of the eruption of Mount Vesuvius.

ROTAS
OPERA
TENET
AREPO
SATOR

Can you also see an important Christian symbol in the acrostic?

The answer is given on page 47.

<table>
<tr><td>

Chapter

3

</td><td>

The Spread of Christianity

</td></tr>
</table>

Christianity began, as we have seen, with a handful of men and women. They shared certain beliefs about Jesus: that he was the anointed one of God, the Messiah – they called him the Son of God; that he had died to deliver people from their sins; and that God had raised him to life on the third day after his crucifixion. How is it that from such small beginnings Christianity has become a religion which is to be found in every country of the world? There are many answers to this question. Some reasons might be:

- the changed lives of the apostles.
- the courage of people like Peter, Paul and Stephen who were ready to die for their faith.
- the readiness of the Jewish Christians to accept Gentiles, otherwise Christianity would have remained a small Jewish movement.
- the dissatisfaction of many people with the other religions of the Greek and Roman world. The gods had become figures of fun, few believed they had any power. Some Gentiles had become 'God-fearers', like Cornelius, worshipping in synagogues. However, they stopped short of becoming converts to Judaism because this might mean loss of Roman citizenship or friends, as well as having to accept circumcision and Jewish dietary laws. Christianity was often unpopular but it did not make these demands, though it offered the worship of one God who seemed to have power and a code of decent conduct.
- Christianity accepted everyone, rich and poor, men and women, even slaves, and taught that everyone was equal – Jesus had died for all humankind.
- the influence of Christian Kings. In 337 CE the Emperor Constantine was baptised shortly before he died. His mother, Helena, was already a Christian. Many people then became Christians because it was the socially respectable thing to do. In Britain in 597 CE the king of Kent, Ethelbert, was converted to Christianity. He used his influence to make his kingdom Christian. This kind of thing often happened, it was part of a subject's loyalty to follow the king's lead. Grand Prince Vladimir of Kiev forced Russia to accept Christianity with his own conversion in 988 CE.

Three hundred years later when Spain, Portugal, Holland, France, Britain and other European countries began colonising the rest of the world, they encouraged missionary work, some more than others, and many of the conquered peoples adopted the language, dress, customs, and religion of the Europeans.

- the flexibility of Christian leaders. As we have already seen, the Council of Jerusalem did not make very heavy demands upon Gentile converts. It never insisted upon one universal language so from very early times the Gospels were translated into local languages from the Greek in which they had originally been written. In the same way local customs were taken over. The best example of this is Christmas. The first mention of it being celebrated is in 336 CE in Rome. The date, 25 December in the west, and almost all the customs attached to the festival have been taken from other religions.

Can you think of any other reasons? Discuss them among yourselves and if they seem worthwhile keep them in your list.

THE WORK OF SOME EARLY MISSIONARIES

The work of the apostles can be referred to as the first phase in the spread of Christianity. The second phase is the work of the early missionaries. The word mission comes from the Latin word meaning sent. Missionaries believe they are sent by God to preach about their religion.

The story of how Christianity reached some places is known for certain. For example, The Acts of the Apostles tells of Paul and Barnabas taking the Christian message to Cyprus for the first time (Acts 13:4) and of Paul doing the same in Malta (Acts 28:1). Later in the same chapter Paul reaches Italy and the capital of the Roman Empire, the great city of Rome. He found Christians there already. No one can be certain how the religion reached there. Roman Christians say Peter took it but this is far from certain.

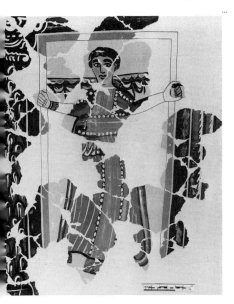

Britain has at least two stories about the coming of Christianity. There is a place called Paulsgrove in Hampshire. Some people in the past said that the apostle Paul landed there and began preaching. Others have said that Joseph of Arimathaea, the man who gave his unused family tomb to be the resting place for the body of Jesus (Luke 23:50), was the first missionary to Britain. Both suggestions are highly unlikely. They show the way in which countries were eager to say that Christianity came to them through a famous person, an apostle if possible.

The owners of Lullingstone Roman Villa in Kent were converted to Christianity in the fourth century CE. The walls of the chapel were painted with Christian symbols and figures, such as this. It shows an early Christian at prayer, arms outstretched. This was the custom at the time. Some clergymen still pray this way at the altar.

St Alban

It is likely that traders or perhaps even soldiers in the imperial army brought Christianity to the Roman province of Britain. The first Christian in Britain about whom much is known was a soldier in the Roman Army called Alban. Although he was not a Christian, he sheltered a priest during a time of persecution. He became a convert and when soldiers came searching for the fugitive Alban put on his cloak and let them believe that they had found their man. The commander soon recognised Alban and threatened him with punishment. Alban replied that he was now a Christian. He was taken before the emperor himself, who was in Britain at the time, and condemned to be executed. He was led out of the town of Verulamium, across the river Ver and up the hill to the north of the town. There he was publicly beheaded. The emperor, probably Severus, died in York in the year 212 CE, so Alban must have been executed a few years earlier. St Alban was the first British martyr to be known by name. The town where he died, Verulamium, is now named St Albans after him.

St Patrick

A century after St Alban, in 306 CE, York was the city from which Constantine set out for Rome in his successful bid to become emperor. From this time onwards there is plenty of evidence of Christianity thriving in Britain but few names until the great St Patrick.

St Patrick was probably born in about the year 390 CE somewhere in the west of Britain (the areas we know as Wales, Somerset and Cumbria today). He was brought up a Christian and may have belonged to quite a well-to-do family as his father seems to have been some kind of local official of the government. However, at 16 he was captured by Irish pirates and carried off to the area of Ireland we now know as County Mayo, where he was enslaved and forced to work as a herdsman. He escaped, returned to Britain and decided that he had a calling to be a priest. After his training he went back to Ireland, even though he could have been executed as a runaway slave. There he was responsible for converting local chieftains, and through them their people, so that Ireland became a centre of Christianity. He died aged about 70.

By the time St Patrick had ended his great work, Britain had ceased to enjoy the protection of the Roman Empire. Peoples and tribes from northern Europe, who were not Christian, settled in Britain. Soon Christianity was only to be found in the west of the island, in Devon, Cornwall, Wales and Cumbria, to give the regions their modern names. The Christians in these areas were too weak to try to convert the rest of Britain – and may not have been very keen to convert their enemies who, doubtless they thought, would end up in hell if they remained unbelievers! It was left to the Irish to begin the reconversion of Britain.

Columba, Aidan and Cuthbert

The reconversion began in 563 CE when Columba, who had set up a number of monasteries in his native Ireland, went with twelve companions to the Scottish island of Iona. He used the island as a base from which to evangelise (spread the Gospel) western Scotland and Northumbria. In 635 CE a monk of Iona named Aidan founded a monastery at Lindisfarne, an island off the coast of Northumbria. This became his headquarters, and after his death in 651 that of a monk called Cuthbert, from where they converted the area between Edinburgh and the Humber.

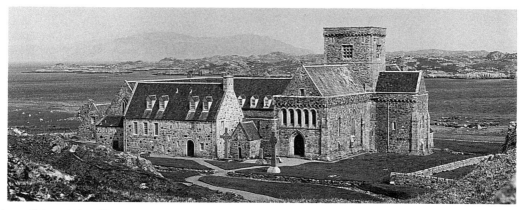

Iona Abbey. It is still a popular place of pilgrimage.

St Augustine

Meanwhile, Pope Gregory I at Rome had heard that there was a northern country which was not Christian. He sent a monk, Augustine, who landed in Kent in 597 CE. He converted its king, Ethelbert, whose wife was already a Christian, and Augustine became the first Archbishop of Canterbury. From Canterbury in the south and Lindisfarne in the north, the English (as they came to be called) were evangelised.

St David

David, the patron saint of Wales, was not so much a missionary as a consolidator of the faith. Wales, like other western parts of the Roman province of Britain, had remained Christian when the rest of the island had been conquered. At the same time that Columba was working from Iona, David was building churches and monasteries, which became centres of learning. Fifty-three churches are dedicated to him in his native land. One of the monasteries that he established was at Mynyw, now known as St Davids.

The ruins of St Non's Chapel, St David's, Dyfed.

St Non was David's mother and tradition states that he was born around 500 CE on the site where her chapel now stands, a mile or so from the cathedral where his relics now lie. His father was a prince of Ceredigion. West Wales was an important centre at this time. It had links with Brittany and the Mediterranean as well as with Ireland, and contacts with Byzantine Christians and the Irish. The legend that St Patrick blessed David while he was still in St Non's womb may be unlikely, for the patron saint of Ireland probably died about the year 460 CE, but there is no reason to doubt that he and other Irish Christians came and went frequently between the two countries. It is also possible that St Non went to Brittany as a missionary after giving birth to St David. She is known there as Dirinon and the chapel containing her tomb is a historic monument.

David was eager to maintain the true Christian faith. A century before his birth a Briton, Pelagius, had caused a stir in Rome by denying the doctrine of original sin. Put very simply, the doctrine is that Adam's disobedience in eating the fruit which Eve offered to him affected all human beings after him. One of the achievements of Jesus was to offer obedience to the Father and so undo the consequences of the sin of Adam. Pelagius claimed that people were free to sin or not sin as they wished. They could save themselves by their own efforts, especially by living highly moral and spiritual lives. Pelagius himself lived a hard, simple life of prayer. The Church realised that the logical consequence of Pelagius's teaching was the belief that the suffering of Jesus was not essential for the redemption of humanity. His views were condemned and he was declared to be a heretic. In his native Britain the ideas taught by Pelagius remained popular and St David spent much time in arguing against them in Wales.

1   Find out what you can about Christianity in your region before about 700 CE. Who were the missionaries?
2   Other countries have their saints – men and women who brought Christianity to them. Choose a country and research the story of its missionaries.

EUROPEAN MISSIONS TO THE REST OF THE WORLD

The second phase of the spread of Christianity might be said to have come to an end when all of the area which we know as Europe had been converted. It had taken a long time. Armenia, just to the south of Russia, may have been the first Christian kingdom, in 301 CE, and Finland was not evangelised until sometime in the twelfth century.

The third phase was the period when European missionaries took the Gospel to other parts of the world. There were already Christians in Ethiopia, the one Christian kingdom in Africa, and a small number in India, as well as many in Persia (now Iran), but until about 1500 the religion was mostly confined to Europe because this was the world that was known to Christians and which they could reach.

A European living in Rome, Canterbury or Venice in 1490 knew that there were people in China and India who were not Christians but it was impossible to reach them. The great Muslim Turkish or Ottoman Empire stood in the way. Further north of this were the massive wastes beyond Russia, with a forbidding climate and inhabitants of legendary ferocity. To the south there were also the Turks, occupying the Mediterranean coast of Africa. Europe was fully known and was Christian. Nothing lay beyond the western ocean (the Atlantic Ocean as we now know it). Then, with the voyage of Columbus in 1492 the situation changed. When the southern tip of Africa was rounded, new countries became accessible to traders, colonisers, plunderers, and missionaries.

Spanish and Portugese Roman Catholics converted the inhabitants of South America and parts of the Caribbean. French and British settlers evangelised some of the people who lived in North America. The Roman Catholic Church met the challenge with a new religious order called the Society of Jesus, or the Jesuits, which was formed in 1534 and approved by Pope Paul III in 1540. Its purpose was to face the problems which the Reformation had caused (see page 29) and evangelise the newly discovered lands. Its founder St Ignatius of Loyola (1491/1495–1556) established missions in India, Malaya, Zaire, Ethiopia, China and Japan. Another of its original members St Francis Xavier (1506–52) set up his headquarters at Goa, in India, in 1542 and in the next ten years made many converts in India, Sri Lanka, and Japan. He died on his way to China.

The Protestant churches were less prepared for the new missionary opportunities which anyway were at first in areas where the Catholics held power or influence. They were also smaller in numbers and divided among themselves. Their opportunity came in the eighteenth and nineteenth century through the Danes, Germans, and British especially; they travelled to India, Africa and the Caribbean. Now there is no country where the Christian message has not been preached.

Read Chapter 11 for further discussion of missionaries.

Chapter 4

Christian Denominations

Before reading this section, think of all the different churches that you know of in the area round your school. How many are there? What are their names?

If you live in a town you might be able to list a dozen or more, as many churches as there are pubs! (Why are there so many pubs?) If you live in a Welsh village you may well find that there are two churches, Baptist probably, and Church in Wales, perhaps. In England they are more likely to be Church of England, Methodist, Roman Catholic, and perhaps others as well. In Scotland there would be Church of Scotland and a similar mix of other churches.

These churches belong to different *denominations* – the groups or churches into which Christianity is divided.

Why are there so many? Not just to give a choice, but because there are different ways of thinking about Christian worship, about how the Church should be organised, and about belief. From its beginnings there has been diversity in Christianity. There were some Jewish Christians, within a few decades of Jesus' ministry, who argued that he was human not divine, an inspired man, rather like their great prophets of the past. These Christians were known as Ebionites. There were Gentiles who found it equally difficult to believe that God could possibly inhabit such a despicable thing as the human body. They believed Jesus was really a spiritual being who appeared to be human. He came to teach mystical knowledge which would deliver them from imprisonment in the body. People who held these kinds of views were called 'gnostics'.

The Apostles' Creed was one attempt to unite all Christians in one faith (see pages 85–7). However, there were also differences in the way that the churches appointed their leaders (bishops). Until the time of the Emperor Constantine, at least, the Christians of Alexandria elected their own bishops without referring the matter to anyone else. Some churches looked for guidance or direction to the bishop of the church at Rome. Eventually, in western Europe, the leadership of the bishop of Rome was accepted. He was after all the successor of St Peter, first bishop there. Many western bishops had been called pope, a word which means father; now it came to be used as the title for the head of the Church in the west. The Church in eastern Europe (Russia, Greece, Turkey, Romania and parts of Yugoslavia) was centred on Byzantium (Constantinople, now Istanbul).

THE GREAT SCHISM, 1054

There had always been two main expressions of Christianity. The eastern Church had never accepted the leadership of the Pope; culturally it belonged to the Greek world which tended to regard the Romans as barbarians. It was not surprising therefore that in 1054 the eastern and western Churches split.

The cause of the split was the words 'and the Son' which the western Church had added to the Nicene Creed (see page 85), 'We believe in the Holy Spirit, the Lord, the giver of life, who proceeds from the Father, and the Son. With Father and Son he is worshipped and glorified.' The eastern Church objected to this because they kept to the statement that had been agreed at the Council of Nicea. The eastern Church became known as the Orthodox church (orthodox describes someone who accepts the established tradition). The Church in the west was unorthodox in their eyes; it had changed the apostolic faith. The western Church eventually came to be known as the Roman Catholic church.

The present Church of St Peter, Rome, was completed in 1626 on the site of Constantine's church. The grave of St Peter probably lies under the High Altar.

Orthodox worship at Trapezny Cathedral. The screen (iconostasis) with icons (see page 56) painted on it can be seen behind the priests.

Note Orthodox churches are not all exactly the same. Some have a gallery from which a choir will sing. Often there will be a dome above the nave with a painting of Christ Pantocrator (ruler of all things) painted on it. There will be a smaller dome over the sanctuary, where the altar stands.

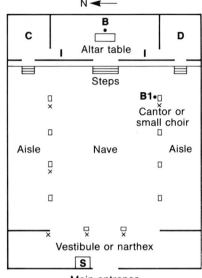

x   Examples of places where individual icons (see page 56) might stand

B   Bishop's throne (sometimes at **B1**)

D   Diaconium (where vestments, service books and priests' robes are kept)

C   Chapel of prothesis where the bread and wine are kept before consecration

I   Iconostasis (screen with icons painted on it)

S   Stand where books and candles can be bought

Plan of an Orthodox Church

In the west Christianity remained united for the next 500 years. From time to time there were individuals or groups of people who questioned the teachings but they were dealt with fairly easily. The individuals were usually intellectuals, teachers in universities. They were convinced to change their views by argument or were dismissed from their posts. At worst they were condemned as heretics (believers in false doctrines), excommunicated (that is, refused the sacraments, see page 49) and put out of the Church. They were often imprisoned, and even put to death. Groups of men and women who opposed the teachings of the Church were a more serious threat. Christian kings usually regarded it as their duty to support the Church, so they used their soldiers to get rid of these groups of heretics.

THE REFORMATION OF THE CHURCH

The relationship between Church and state worked well until the sixteenth century. However, there was now some feeling that the taxes paid to Rome should remain in England, Scotland, France or Sweden, or whichever country they were collected from, instead of going to Italy, where they did not seem to be put to good use. Often they were used to pay for the Pope's wars or palaces. They might as well pay for the wars and palaces of the English or French king! There were also many other criticisms of the Church and its representatives, of monasteries which took the land of villagers to turn it into grazing for sheep, of priests who were scarcely literate enough to read the Mass, for example.

The challenge to the authority of the Pope built up gradually during the fourteenth and fifteenth centuries, until it found a champion in a young German monk, Martin Luther.

Martin Luther (1483–1546)

Martin Luther was a devout priest, deeply concerned by the state of the Church. He had visited Rome and been very disturbed by what he saw. There seemed to be more interest in money and luxurious living than in caring for the poor and needy. The crisis came when he was back in Germany and heard a Pope's representative selling Indulgences (papers granting the purchaser pardon and forgiveness). The Church has always had a right and duty to forgive sins. Jesus once said to his disciples, 'If you forgive any man's sins, they stand forgiven; if you pronounce them unforgiven, unforgiven they remain' (John 20:23). The Church is the successor of the first followers of Jesus. However, this man was selling forgiveness, or so it seemed to Martin Luther. He was telling people that if they bought an Indulgence, their sins would be forgiven. They could even buy such pardons on behalf of dead relatives. Some people put the preacher's words into a rhyme:

> As soon as the money in the coffer rings,
> The soul from Hell's torment springs.

D. Martin Luther.

Luther was disturbed by what he saw. Poor people were being exposed to emotional blackmail, persuaded to part with the little money they had to release a child who had died in infancy, or a parent, from the torment of Hell. He had also read Paul's words in the New Testament, 'He shall gain life who is justified through faith' (Romans 1:17), quoting the Jewish prophet Habakkuk (Habakkuk 2:4). He had concluded that there was no need to pay for forgiveness, since Jesus had already paid the price by his death. All that was needed was faith in Jesus. In the manner of scholars of his day Luther decided to seek a debate on the subject of Indulgences but Church officials were in no mood to have this valuable source of income challenged. The money was needed urgently to build the new church of St Peter in Rome. Martin Luther was summoned before one of the Pope's representatives because of his disobedience in challenging the teachings of the Church. Realising what this might mean (imprisonment or even death), he fled instead to a place called Wittenburg, to seek the protection of its ruler. A debate did take place eventually, but it was clear that Luther's protests were not going to be heeded.

From challenging Indulgences he moved on to questioning the authority of the Pope himself. The German princes did not all side with the Church, many of them supported Luther, who was allowed to remain free and spread his views. He and his supporters regarded themselves as reformers. They did not wish to destroy the Church but to bring it back to the faith of the Apostles, which they believed it had neglected.

What Martin Luther began is known as the Reformation. He, and those after him who have shared his ideas, are called Protestants.

Why was the name Protestant given to those who followed Martin Luther? Find out more about Luther, John Calvin and other reformers of this period.

The Church before the Middle Ages had been international and that which owed its allegiance to the Pope remained international. The majority in the west held to the traditions of the Roman Catholic Church, and still do. It remains the largest Church in the world, with the Orthodox Church second. Many Protestant Churches became international. One of the best known of these is the Church of England (the Anglican Church), which kept many of the traditions of the Roman Church, including bishops, but replaced the Pope with the sovereign in temporal matters. A gathering, known as a convocation, of archbishops, bishops and priests was to decide on spiritual issues and guide that part of the Church's life.

The Protestant Church continued to split into many denominations.

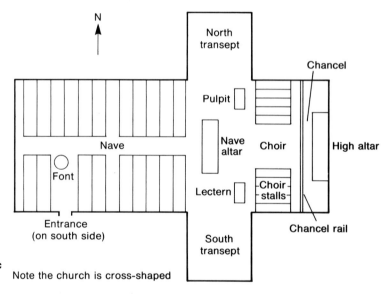

Plan of a Roman Catholic or Anglican Church   Note the church is cross-shaped

Presbyterians

The reformers had successfully challenged the authority of the Pope. They had to find something or someone to put in his place to decide matters of belief. They decided that the Bible should be the authority. However, when they began to study the Bible, especially the New Testament in the original Greek, they started to question many other things which had long been taken for granted. For example, there were the Greek words *presbyteros* (Acts 14:23) and *episkopos* (Acts 20:28), which were understood to mean bishop, but the words really meant 'elder' and 'overseer'. Perhaps the leaders of churches in New Testament times were not the powerful secular, as well as religious, rulers that they were in the days of Martin Luther.

Some Christians, who became known as Presbyterians, rejected bishops altogether, saying that the Church should be governed by elders through a series of meetings called courts. These elders were elected by the local congregation to assist the minister but some would also represent their congregation at other courts responsible for the government of the Church at district or national level.

In Scotland the national Church eventually became Presbyterian in form, following the practice of John Calvin in Geneva. It had no bishops. Government was by a gathering of ministers and elders, called a General Assembly. Its leading figure, the Moderator, is appointed for one year only.

The Society of Friends

There were Christians who felt that, having freed the Church from the authority of the Pope, they did not want to have the king or queen as ruler instead. They argued that the only head of the Church was Jesus who had promised that, 'For where two or three have met together in my name, I am there among them' (Matthew 18:20). They rejected popes, bishops and state rulers, appointed their own ministers, and interpreted the Bible as they understood it, guided by the Holy Spirit.

One group in England went even further. In 1647 George Fox (1624–91) became convinced that Jesus spoke directly to him as an inner voice of enlightenment. He began to preach about this direct experience which was far more convincing than biblical quotations or the arguments of theologians (learned specialists in the study of Christian beliefs) or the sacraments. Those who followed him called themselves Friends of Truth, and are now known as members of the Society of Friends, or Quakers.

Baptists

Some Christians, who based their faith and religious practices solely on the Bible, came to the conclusion that the New Testament only supported the baptism of adult believers. The practice which had grown up of baptising infants had no scriptual justification and should be rejected. Thus, in the seventeenth century, the Baptist churches came into existence.

Methodists

In the eighteenth century, there were two brothers who were members of the Church of England but were concerned that it was becoming lazy, and indifferent to the needs of the people, just like the Roman Church of Luther's day. They were John and Charles Wesley.

John Wesley travelled the length and breadth of the British Isles, mostly on horseback, preaching to anyone who would listen to him. His enthusiasm upset some vicars who would not have him or his converts in their churches, though others welcomed him. The name 'Methodist' was first given to the Wesleys and their friends at Oxford University, but it was later applied to those who accepted the message and disciplined way of life which John Wesley preached. In some countries the Methodist Church has bishops, in Britain it does not.

Redruth Methodist Church, Cornwall.

F Portable font on communion table
C Cloakrooms

Note There is no altar and the communion table does not face east. Not all churches are exactly the same as this plan.

*The terms non-conformist and free church are both used to refer to Protestant churches who do not follow the form of worship contained in the *Book of Common Prayer*, adopted by the Church of England in 1662.

Plan of a Non-conformist, or Free, Church*

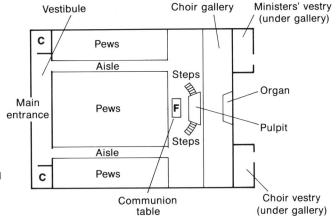

The Salvation Army

The Methodists themselves became less concerned than they had been about the poor in the great industrial cities which emerged in Britain in the nineteenth century. One of them, William Booth (1829–1912) left the Methodists in 1861 and established the Christian Mission. Out of this developed the Salvation Army (see page 38).

It is estimated that there are now over 2000 denominations in the world. Whether this includes the Jehovah's Witnesses, or the Church of Latter Day Saints (Mormons), which some Christians would not accept as Christian, is uncertain.

1   The diagram below is a simple family tree of the *main* Christian denominations which are found in the UK today. Make one of your own neighbourhood or town and include the dates when various local Christian groups began to meet for worship. A few things to look for are:
   ● Where did the Roman Catholics go when the parish church became Anglican?
   ● When did the first Baptists or Independents (Congregationalists) hold their separate meetings and where?
   ● Did John Wesley visit your part of the world? Do his journals contain any interesting stories about it, if he did?
   ● When was the Salvation Army Citadel built?
   ● When was the Kingdom Hall of the Jehovah's Witnesses built?
   ● Find out what you can about the United Reformed Church in your district, if there is one.

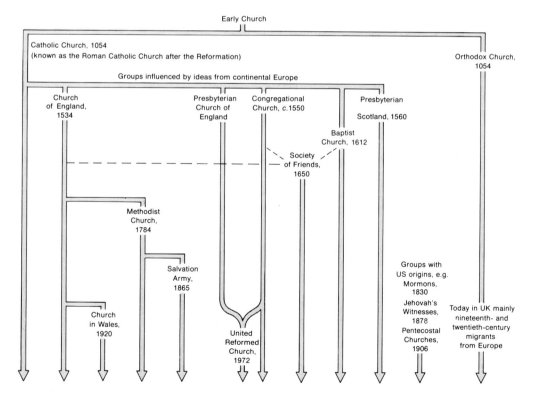

2   The past is interesting but it is the present and future that really matter. Try to discover what these different denominations do today.

<table>
<tr><td>

Chapter

5

</td><td>

Christian Worship

</td></tr>
</table>

In this chapter we shall look at what people do when they worship but we need to begin by asking what worship is and why some people feel a need or desire to worship God.

?

1 What do you think worship is? Write down a few ideas and discuss them with the person next to you. Then share your results with the rest of the class.
2 Collect a few dictionary definitions of worship and compare them with your own suggestions.

WHAT IS WORSHIP?

Worship is hard to define and describe; in this respect it is a bit like beauty or love. It contains an element of wonder. It makes us gasp and catch our breath. Cor! Phew! and Fantastic! may be some of the exclamations we find ourselves making. There is also something fascinating about worship. Time seems to stand still, we forget the people around us and all our attention is given to the object of worship. There is also a sense of being in the presence of someone or something greater than ourselves which overwhelms us. Yet the worshipper is attracted to this being or power, as well as being struck dumb by it.

People offer worship to God because of this attraction. They feel that however awesome or mysterious God is, God nevertheless wishes to have a relationship with them, and they want to have a relationship with God – for all kinds of reasons.

?

Think of reasons why a person might want a relationship with God. Write them down – we will return to them later.

Wonder, fascination and a sense of being overwhelmed are not the things which might always strike someone on joining a group of Christians at worship. It might appear much more humdrum, as many familiar things do, but they would probably be present just beneath the surface in the form of the architecture of the building, in the words of the songs (called hymns) which the congregation sing, in the words read from the Bible, in the actions of those conducting the service, or in the talk (sermon) given by the minister, preacher or priest. They have to be looked for and listened for. The worshipper has to make an effort. As one Christian put it, 'Come, not to express an opinion, but to seek a Presence.'

WHY WORSHIP?

'Thank God for Jesus': you may have read these words on a sticker at the back of a car, or on a notice outside a church. They sum up the main reason for worship for many Christians. Christian worship places a strong emphasis upon thanking God, and upon Jesus. A service will often begin with a hymn of praise, not because God wants to be told how wonderful he is or to remind the worshipper but to help the worshipper express the awe and wonder which he or she feels in consciously entering God's presence. A very popular hymn begins:

> All people that on earth do dwell,
> Sing to the Lord with cheerful voice,
> Him serve with mirth, his praise forthtell,
> Come ye, before him, and rejoice.

It was written 400 years ago so the language may seem a little strange. In those days 'mirth' meant joy, not laughter or fun, but the meaning remains clear, and the fourth verse lists four reasons why God should be worshipped:

> For why? The Lord our God is good,
> His mercy is forever sure,
> His truth at all times firmly stood,
> And shall from age to age endure.

William Kettle

Write down as many reasons as you can why Christians worship God, including those in the fourth verse of 'All people that on earth do dwell' in modern English!

Singing hymns in a Roman Catholic church – St Mary of the Angels, Bayswater, London.

HOW DO CHRISTIANS WORSHIP?

Have you ever wondered why Christians sing hymns when they worship God? You might if you ever hear poor singing or the embarrassed murmurings which pass for singing when only six or seven people may be present in a church which could hold 600. You might too if you had visited a meeting for worship held by the Society of Friends where there would be no singing (see pages 31, 38 and 43). There are three possible reasons for singing hymns:

- it is natural to sing when people are happy
- it is part of the tradition (Christians have always done it)
- it was part of the Jewish tradition from which Christians came. The hymn 'All people that on earth do dwell' is based upon Psalm 100. If you look in that part of the Bible which formed the scripture of the first Christians, the Old Testament as Christians now call it, you will find there are 150 Psalms; they were used in the Jerusalem Temple and the synagogues which Jesus and his disciples attended. Some Christians believe that they are the only songs that it is appropriate to sing in church.

There were four main elements in the worship of the early Christians. Three of them would have been shared in by Jesus himself. These were:

- the singing of hymns, the Psalms of the Bible, to which Christians were soon adding their own compositions in praise of Jesus
- praying
- preaching
- the breaking of bread (Acts 2:42).

All four are part of Christian worship today, though the first Jewish Christians might not easily recognise them. For example, they probably prayed standing up, as the Jewish custom still is. They might take a moment or two to realise that Christians kneeling, or sitting with bowed heads, are doing the same thing. It was also the practice to gather for worship every day, not once a week.

If you were to go anywhere in the world you would find Christian worship divided into two main types, despite all kinds of variations. One places the emphasis on the *Eucharist* and the other on the *sermon*, though as we shall see the two are frequently combined.

The Eucharist

Eucharist, Holy Communion, Lord's Supper and Breaking of Bread are different names for the same kind of worship – an activity based on the meal which Jesus shared with some of his disciples on the night of his arrest. He may have done something like it many times before. In Luke's Gospel (24:13–35) there is an account of the risen Jesus catching up with two of his disciples who were grief-stricken because they knew of the crucifixion but were not aware of its sequel (see page 10). He went with them to where they were spending the night and shared a meal with them. They had not recognised him at

first but, Luke writes, they later told other disciples that 'he had been recognised by them at the breaking of the bread.' Some mannerism, some word perhaps, opened their eyes.

The story seems to suggest that 'breaking bread' was a part of the life with Jesus, not surprisingly, for the sharing of food is a universal way of expressing friendship, as well as being very important in Judaism. Sometimes it is suggested that the Last Supper was a Passover meal. In Luke 22:15 Jesus says to his friends during the meal, 'How I have longed to eat this Passover with you before my death.'

However, the real importance for Christians lies in some other words which he spoke. The apostle Paul, writing to Christians at Corinth, complained that they were turning the Lord's Supper, as he called it, into a meal which drew attention to class divisions rather than Christian unity. He reminded them that this was no ordinary meal, they should remember its significance and behave accordingly. Paul wrote:

> For the tradition which I handed on to you came to me from the Lord himself: that the Lord Jesus, on the night of his arrest, took bread and, after giving thanks to God, broke it and said: 'This is my body, which is for you; do this as a memorial of me.' In the same way, he took the cup after supper, and said: 'This cup is the new covenant sealed by my blood. Whenever you drink it, do this as a memorial of me.' For every time you eat this bread and drink the cup, you proclaim the death of the Lord, until he comes.

> I Corinthians 11:23-6

This is the oldest record of the words which Jesus spoke at the meal, written by Paul about 20 years before the first of the Gospel accounts. The Gospels do not mention the command, 'Do this as a memorial' (some versions of Luke do, but they may have been altered to match the words written by Paul). It is these words which provide the reason why some Christians celebrate the Eucharist. They are obeying the command of Jesus.

The words 'This is my body' and 'This is my blood' have provoked the fiercest arguments among Christians about the Lord's Supper. Sometimes they have even led to Christians imprisoning or killing one another. What did Jesus really intend his disciples to think when he uttered these words? For many centuries Christians agreed that the words meant precisely what they said. In the service, when the words of Jesus were spoken, the bread and wine became the actual body and blood of Jesus, though the appearance of bread and wine remained. At an assembly of the Church in 1215, known as the Fourth Lateran Council, this interpretation, known as the doctrine of *transubstantiation*, was decreed to be the official teaching of the Church. Although the Orthodox Church had separated from the Roman Church by now, it shared the same view on this matter.

Not all Christians hold this belief. At the opposite extreme are those who note the word 'memorial' in the passage written by Paul. They stress the idea of remembrance or calling to mind, rather in the way that people commemorate the end of a war, or the anniversary of the death of a loved one, or Christmas or Easter, not casually but with feeling and respect.

Martin Luther (see page 29) put forward the idea of *consubstantiation*, affirming that after the consecration of the bread and wine they exist as both the body and blood of Jesus *and* as bread and wine.

Two famous Christian groups or denominations do not celebrate the Lord's Supper at all; they are the Salvation Army and the Society of Friends (Quakers). Much of the work of the Salvation Army has been among people with drink problems. To offer an alcoholic communion wine seemed to be inviting more trouble. However, it goes even further and rejects baptism too, refusing to believe that spiritual benefits are channelled through such means. God reaches the sinner as *he* wishes and not in special ways. The Society of Friends shares the same kind of belief – that God's love, mercy, and forgiveness are not confined to special times, occasions and rituals. Every meal should be regarded as a reminder of the Last Supper because Jesus is always present in the hearts of believers.

A statement by Friends in America says:

> The absence from Friends' worship of the outward observance of the Lord's Supper and of Baptism is due to the emphasis on the reality of inward experience. Friends are aware of the power of a true, inward baptism of the Holy Spirit; in the meeting for worship at its best, they know direct communion with God and fellowship with one another. These experiences make the outward rites seem unnecessary to some and even a hindrance to full attainment of the spiritual experiences which are symbolised.

While recognising the help that has come through the outward forms to countless generations of Christians, Friends seek to experience without symbols the essentially inward and continuing source of the sacraments. Friends affirm the sacramental nature of the whole of life when it is under the healing of the spirit.

Philadelphia Faith and Practice, USA, 1978

The names which Christians use for the service give some clue to where they place the emphasis. Eucharist means thanksgiving. At the Last Supper Jesus took the bread and gave thanks before sharing it with his friends (Luke 22:19). Christians give thanks for the life and death of Jesus and the gift of salvation which they have received as the result of his sacrifice. Roman Catholic Christians especially have the idea of sacrifice strongly in mind when they think about the Eucharist. In a sense the sacrifice of Jesus on the cross is re-enacted at each Eucharist. They also use the word Mass for the service. It comes from some words at the end of the celebration, the dismissal, *missa est* in Latin, the language used by that Church for many centuries.

Members of the Orthodox Church will use Eucharist or Mass but also refer to the service as the Divine Liturgy. Anglicans may speak of Holy Communion as well as Eucharist or Mass. The most popular Protestant names are Last Supper, Lord's Supper, Communion (sometimes Holy Communion) or the Breaking of Bread, the emphasis being on the meal and remembrance rather than the phrase 'body and blood'. Jehovah's Witnesses use the word 'Memorial' and commemorate the Last Supper annually on the date of its anniversary after sunset on the 14th Nisan, the date of the Jewish Passover as observed by Jesus in Jerusalem.

1   Conduct a survey of all the church notice-boards in your district. Make a list of the names used by each church for the service based on the Last Supper. How frequently are these services held?
2   List as many reasons as you can why Roman Catholic churches consider the Mass so important that they offer it every day.
3   Suggest reasons why some denominations hold communion services only monthly, or even annually.

In the Middle Ages so much importance was given to the Mass, celebrated by priests in Latin (a language which most people could not understand) that some Christians, when they broke away in protest and formed what came to be known as Protestant Churches (see page 30), held a service of the Lord's Supper only once a year. They felt that the command of Jesus to 'Do this as a memorial' should be obeyed but disagreed with the idea that it did not matter what kind of life you lived, as long as you attended the Mass your sins would be forgiven.

The service which we have been discussing began as a meal, the Last Supper, and continued to be one for some years, but Paul, in his first letter to the Christians of Corinth, was critical of the way in which it had become very unchristian with some people getting drunk and the poor receiving scarcely any food at all; apparently everyone brought their own food and ate it themselves, without even waiting until everyone had assembled. Paul paints a pretty dreadful picture, 'The result is that when you meet as a congregation, it is impossible for you to eat the Lord's Supper, because each of you is in such a hurry to eat his own, and while one goes hungry another has too much to drink' (I Corinthians 11:20–1).

For this reason and also because rumours circulated that Christian love feasts, as they were sometimes called (the Greek word is *agapé*, were really 'love-ins' or orgies, the meal was soon replaced by a symbolic sharing of consecrated bread and wine. Anyone going to a communion service in a church today, whatever it is called and however frequently or rarely it takes place, should not expect even a one-course meal.

Receiving the elements

Elements is the name given to the consecrated bread and wine which a communicant (the person taking part in the communion service) receives. Although denominations often have their own special traditions and reasons for receiving the elements in a particular way, many variations can be found. For example, in Anglican churches it may be most usual to be given a wafer representing the bread, actual bread might be preferred or sometimes a loaf may be passed round for each communicant to tear off a small piece to eat. Sometimes the wafer may be placed in the communicant's hand, or it may be put directly into his or her mouth by the priest.

1   The photographs on pages 37, 39 and 40 show the receiving of the elements in different traditions.

a)   Study each picture and write a brief description of how the elements are being received.

b)   Discuss each picture in a group and see how many reasons you can think of for the way in which the elements are being received. It may be religious, related to some of the ideas already mentioned in this chapter, or it may simply be functional, having more to do with convenience than belief.

2   Hymns are often sung during communion services. Read the verses which are given below and try to decide what ideas about the Eucharist the authors had in mind. If you can get hold of some hymn-books you might collect a few more examples of each type.

We come obedient to thy word,
To feast on heavenly food,
Our meat the body of the Lord,
Our drink his precious blood.

Thee we adore O hidden Saviour,
Who in thy sacrament dost deign to be,
Both flesh and spirit at thy presence fail,
Yet here thy presence we devoutly hail.

Jesus to thy table led,
Now let every heart be fed,
With the true and living bread.
When we taste the mystic wine,
Of thine outpoured love the sign,
Fill our hearts with love divine.

Bread of the world in mercy broken,
Wine of the soul in mercy shed,
By whom the words of life were spoken,
And in whose death our sins are dead,
Look on the heart by sorrow broken,
Look on the tears by sinners shed,
And be thy feast to us the token,
That by thy grace our souls are fed.

Author of life divine,
Who hast a table spread,
Furnished with mystic wine,
And everlasting bread,
Preserve the life thyself hath given,
And feed and train us up for heaven.

What do these verses tell you about other things which Christians think of during the communion service?

3   Ask the clergy of a local church if you may visit it so that he could simulate a Eucharist. (Be careful to use the appropriate name when you make your request, and learn the correct vocabulary of the denomination before you go.)

The Service of the Word

In Roman Catholic, Orthodox, and Anglican Churches, the main service is the Eucharist or Mass, though they do have other kinds of services and often scripture readings, a sermon, and the singing of hymns form part of the celebration of the Lord's Supper. However, as we have seen, some denominations, mostly Protestant, will hold less frequent eucharists, perhaps monthly, quarterly, or even annually. For these the normal Sunday services will focus on the reading and interpretation of scripture, that is, the reading of the Bible followed by a talk, called a *sermon*, in which the passage is explained and its message related to the life of Christians today. This is known as the 'service of the Word'. 'The Word of God' is a phrase which some Christians use to describe the Bible. The emphasis is on reading, and preaching, that is upon *words*, so to call it the service of the Word is quite appropriate.

The shape or order of such services varies immensely, but the following outline is fairly basic, though it actually comes from a Scottish order of service:

> *Introductory sentences* (the minister calls upon the congregation to join in worship and probably reads a few verses from the Bible)
> *Hymn*
> *Prayer*
> *Bible reading* (Old Testament)
> *Hymn*
> *Bible reading* (New Testament)
> *Notices* (of coming events, meetings and services)
> *Offertory* (the collection of money gifts from the congregation and prayer dedicating them to the service of God)
> *Prayers* (usually including the Lord's Prayer)
> *Sermon*
> *Hymn*
> *Benediction* (prayer commending the congregation to God's care)

Sometimes the 'Word' is stressed at such services by a number of other features. The notice-board outside the church may announce 'the preacher next Sunday' and this may also be mentioned in the notices. The hymns may be based upon the Bible. A very important contribution of Scottish Christianity to worship in the English-speaking world has been the rendering of the psalms into poetry. (The psalms are a collection of songs used in Jewish worship found in the Old Testament.) One of the most famous and popular hymns begins:

> The Lord's my shepherd, I'll not want:
> He makes me down to lie
> In pastures green; he leadeth me
> The quiet waters by.

This is based on Psalm 23 and comes from the Scottish Psalter of 1650. In Scotland these compositions, known as metrical psalms, have been very frequently used since they were published, and help to ensure that worship is strongly biblical.

A visitor to a Free Church of Scotland service would not find the word hymn used at all. God's praises would be sung using the kind of psalms mentioned in the previous paragraph. There would be no organ, piano, or other musical instruments. A precentor would give the note and lead the singing, sometimes line-by-line, with the congregation following. They would sit for the psalms and stand for the prayers which would not come from a book. The minister would offer the prayer which the Holy Spirit moved him to make, not something previously thought out or read from a book.

In the Anglican service of Matins (or Morning Prayer) a psalm and other passages from the Bible are sung, such as the song which Zechariah composed to celebrate the birth of his son John the Baptist (Luke 1:68–79), and the song of Mary, known as the *Magnificat* (Luke 1:46–55), which she sang when she was told that she would be the mother of Jesus.

The Society of Friends

One other act of worship which must be mentioned is that practised by the Society of Friends, also known as Quakers (see page 31). They sing no hymns in their meeting for worship in the UK, although in the USA they sometimes do. They will gather in reflective silence and no one will speak unless he or she feels prompted to by the Holy Spirit. Such a meeting may last for an hour without a word having been spoken, or several people may stand up during that time and share their thoughts with the meeting. Someone might pray, another might take the Bible which will be lying on a table in the centre of the group, and read a passage, perhaps saying a few words about it afterwards and then sitting down. The Christians who began the movement disliked the formality of worship in the churches they attended. Hymns seemed to be sung without conviction. The preacher stood up and mouthed a sermon which contained little thought and might have been borrowed from someone else. The prayers were read but did not come from the heart. The men and women who became Friends criticised this kind of worship, sometimes arguing with the minister during the service, and then separated to form gatherings of their own in which they stressed waiting upon the Holy Spirit.

? Give as many reasons as you can why Friends do not celebrate the Eucharist.

Meeting for worship at the Friends Meeting House, Sutton, Surrey.

The Charismatic Movement

Among all the groups which have been mentioned there has been a recent development known as the Charismatic Movement. Being possessed by the Holy Spirit has always been a feature of Christianity and was part of its parent faith, Judaism. King David was moved to dance before the Ark during a victory parade, and prophets were inspired to speak the word of God. In charismatic worship men or women may be moved by the Holy Spirit to speak spontaneously to the congregation. Someone may speak in tongues, that is make utterances in a language which is unknown to linguists, but is the result of the Holy Spirit taking control of the speaker.

Spontaneous acts of healing may also form part of the service. This kind of experience is not to be found in most acts of worship, but examples are to be found in most denominations worldwide. The Acts of the Apostles contains many descriptions of worship or other activities when the Holy Spirit took over the life of the community and amazing things happened. The most famous example is to be found in Acts, the story of Pentecost (see page 67). Some churches in which this kind of worship is experienced are called *Pentecostal* for that reason.

The Housechurch Movement

Living religions must keep evolving and changing to respond to the environment in which they exist. This does not necessarily mean that the message alters, but the presentation may. At the time of writing the development which seems to be attracting most attention in Britain is the Housechurch Movement which may have about 30 000 members. These are, for the most part, Protestant Christians who have become dissatisfied with the main stream

A Housechurch group.

traditional churches and are looking for a fellowship which is more intimate and personal. They therefore meet in one another's homes to study the scriptures, sing hymns, pray and break bread. They are returning to a pattern found in the New Testament. Often a number of men (elders) are elected from among the group to organise and govern it. The groups usually begin as spontaneous, independent assemblies of a few people, perhaps less than ten in many cases, but as they have grown and expanded links have been established between some of the housegroups and a new church, or denomination, may be emerging. As their numbers are growing so much, some groups rent accommodation, such as school halls, or build their own churches.

?

1   Explain the following words using a sentence for each:
   a)   worship   e)   offertory
   b)   hymn   f)   elements
   c)   sermon   g)   charismatic
   d)   holy communion

2   Select the most appropriate name for the Last Supper for the following:
   a)   Baptists   e)   Presbyterians
   b)   Roman Catholics   f)   Methodists
   c)   Greek Orthodox   g)   Anglicans
   d)   Jehovah's Witnesses   h)   United Reformed

3   Assemble a register of local churches listing:
   • its name and address, e.g. St Michael's, Station Road
   • the title of its minister or clergyman, e.g. vicar, curate, deacon
   • times of the Sunday services
   • names given to the services, especially the Eucharist
   • other listed activities, e.g. Boys' Brigade, Tuesday, 7 p.m.
   (You may find it useful to obtain the monthly magazine which many churches produce to help you assemble the information. Some activities may not clearly fit into the categories listed; you may need to find out more details from someone at the church to help you decide.)
   a)   Which denomination has the least churches?
   b)   Which denomination has the most churches?

4   Produce a photograph album showing pictures of the outsides, notice-boards, and insides of as many churches as possible, especially local ones. Add plans of the interior of the buildings.

<table>
<tr><td>**Chapter**
6</td><td># *The Lord's Prayer*</td></tr>
</table>

When Jesus' disciples asked him to teach them to pray, as John the Baptist and other spiritual teachers did, he did not tell them when, or how, in any detail. He simply told them to go away into a quiet place. Some people used prayer as a way of showing off. They wrapped their prayer shawls around them and stood praying for a long time, with loud voices, hoping to attract notice and the praise of passers-by or other members of the synagogue, who would think they were great men of prayer. Jesus said that such people would get the reward they were seeking. The attention-seekers would receive attention. However, those who wished to be heard by God should speak privately to him.

Jesus did give his disciples a prayer to say, the Lord's Prayer. There are two versions of it in the New Testament (Matthew 6:9–13 and Luke 11:2–4) and slightly different forms of it are used in church services. The most popular English rendering seems to be:

> Our Father, who art in heaven, hallowed by thy name;
> Thy kingdom come, thy will be done, on earth as it is in heaven.
> Give us this day our daily bread, and forgive us our trespasses,
>   as we forgive them that trespass against us.
> Lead us not into temptation, but deliver us from evil;
> For thine is the kingdom, the power, and the glory, for ever, and ever,
> Amen.

(*Note*: Amen means 'let it be so'.)

Compare this with versions you might find in other liturgies, and with translations in the Bible. One used in Scotland, for example, says, 'Forgive us our debts, as we forgive our debtors', which may seem more sensible than talking about 'trespasses'. The New English Bible has 'Forgive us the wrong we have done, as we forgive those who have wronged us' (Matthew) and 'Forgive us our sins, for we too forgive those who have done us wrong' (Luke). It is important to try to find out what Jesus really said and meant because he was not giving the disciples something to repeat thoughtlessly. He was probably giving them a *model*. When they prayed, the disciples should be concerned about the kinds of things which he had mentioned. However, because these were the words which Jesus taught them, and may have used himself, they came to be so special that they are used in almost every Christian service.

?

1 Learn the Lord's Prayer in the form which you prefer.
2 Give your reasons for your choice.
3 If you are bilingual in a language such as Arabic or French or learning a second language such as Welsh, German, or Hindi, try to discover the form used by Christians when they are worshipping in those languages, and translate it. Compare it with English versions. If you cannot find the words used in worship it should be possible to obtain New Testaments in these languages and compare the verses in them.
4 List the seven or eight points which Jesus seems to be saying that a Christian should have in mind when he is praying.
5 Why do you think Jesus considered these to be important?
6 Write the Matthew and Luke versions side by side, putting each new idea or point on a separate line. You will see that the order is similar. Why do you think Jesus chose to list the items in this particular way?
7 What does the Lord's Prayer teach Christians about prayer?

The Lord's Prayer Puzzle

The Lord's Prayer is sometimes known as the *Pater Noster* because these are the first two words of the Latin version which Christians used for centuries. In an earlier chapter (page 22) you were given a Lord's Prayer acrostic. By rearranging the letters it is possible to spell out *Pater Noster* twice:

```
                α
                P
                A
                T
                E
                R
α P A T E R N O S T E R ω
                O
                S
                T
                E
                R
                ω
```

The acrostic found in Cirencester, Gloucestershire, in 1868. The most popular theory is that it was a secret Christian sign, but no one knows for certain.

The letters, α and ω are the first and last letters of the Greek alphabet, *alpha* (A) and *omega*(O). They are often used of Jesus, especially as victor over death and evil. In Revelation 21:6 the 'One who is seated on the throne', says, 'I am alpha and omega, the beginning and the end'. The form of the cross both in the puzzle and in the Pater Noster solution may be more than coincidental.

```
R O T A S
O P E R A
T E N E T
A R E P O
S A T O R
```

Means of Grace

Grace is a very important word which Christians often use. In a dictionary it might be explained as help or assistance, but it is far more than that.

Jesus once told a story of a young man who decided to leave home. His father was fit, and he had an older brother. There did not seem much of a future for him working on the family farm. So, he asked his father for the share of the inheritance that would be his one day and set out to find what life had to offer elsewhere. To cut a long story short, things went terribly wrong and he ended up looking after pigs. At this point he came to his senses and realised that things must be better at home even if his father only employed him as a servant. The son returned to his father who did not throw his foolishness in his face or remind him of the money that he had wasted, but gave him a party and new clothes. (You can read the account in Luke 15:11–24.)

This story explains what Christians mean by grace better than any dictionary. The father is God and the way he treated his son is grace. 'Undeserved love' is perhaps the best phrase we can use to explain it. Some Christians say there must be an element of human effort and deserving. (The son in the story had to set off home and be ready to eat humble pie.) Others stress the line in the story which says 'While he was still a long way off his father saw him, and his heart went out to him', in other words his father was already looking out for him and probably had been ever since the son left home. Christians who emphasise the father's love in this way attach little importance to the son's efforts and speak of their own religious experience of God's undeserved love helping them to live their lives day by day.

Grace, for a Christian, is not only love, it also includes power. The father in the story had the ability to help his son, to give him back his self-respect and his place in the family. God's grace is the kind of love which gives people the strength to live as Christians. God's undeserved love is there all the time, and many Christians would say it is available to everyone whether they are Christians, people of other faiths, or of no faith at all. God's love cannot be restricted by human beliefs or actions. In the New Testament grace is often linked with the power of the Holy Spirit, who often behaved in a random manner and in ways which seem unusual to most people today, especially in Europe and North America.

Christians are often aware of God's grace in the whole of their lives but especially when they pray, read the Bible or share in worship. They have come to speak of special ways in which grace comes to them which they call *sacraments*, means of grace.

THE SACRAMENTS

The Roman Catholic and Orthodox churches came to accept seven sacraments, or means of grace: Baptism, Confirmation, the Eucharist, Penance, Unction, Marriage and Orders. The Anglican and Protestant denominations only recognise the sacraments of Baptism and the Eucharist as essential. These, they say, were the only ones which Jesus mentioned and told his followers to observe.

Baptism

This is the act of initiation into the Christian Church, either as an infant or, in some denominations, upon personal confession of faith in Jesus (see page 31).

Confirmation

Confirmation is a ritual which is performed to confirm the sacrament of Baptism. It completes it in two ways. First, the Holy Spirit which the baby had received at baptism is conveyed more fully. Secondly, the baptism vows had been made on behalf of the child at infant baptism, now the person makes them himself or herself.

At confirmation people receive the gift of the Holy Spirit through the laying on of hands and become full members of the Church. What is the status of the man performing the ceremony?

The Eucharist

The shared act performed in response to Jesus' command during the last meal which he took with his disciples on the night before his death, when he said, 'Do this as a memorial of me' (I Corinthians 11:24-6) (see pages 36–41).

Penance

When Christians sincerely repent of sins which they have committed and wish to do God's will, they receive grace to help them carry out their intentions. Penance is the formal act of confessing sins to a priest and receiving absolution (forgiveness).

Extreme Unction

This is the practice of anointing a sick person with oil so that they might be healed by God's grace. It is performed on dying Christians so that they may have the power to die in peace and for the forgiveness of sins.

Marriage

Christian marriage is regarded as a sacrament.

Orders

This is the ritual by which a person is consecrated deacon or priest (see page 52). Only a bishop can perform this sacrament.

Priests perform all these sacraments except orders. A deacon, however, may conduct baptisms, weddings and give Extreme Unction. In circumstances where an infant may die, anyone who is baptised may baptise the baby. This could also apply to an unbaptised adult in a similar situation.

Clergy

Clergy are people specially ordained (appointed) to conduct religious services and perform the sacraments. Many Christians believe that this was originally a right and privilege bestowed on the apostles by Jesus, and which they in turn passed on to their successors, and which has continued until the present day. This is known as the apostolic succession. The Pope, Orthodox Patriarchs and the archbishops belong to this.

The Apostolic Succession

Jesus had many followers or disciples but twelve of them were chosen to be his constant companions. These, with the exception of Judas who committed suicide and was replaced by Matthias, came to be known as apostles when Jesus sent them out to preach the Gospel (see page 15). Apostle means 'one who is sent'. Twelve was a significant number. There were twelve tribes which made up the Jewish nation. The first task of the apostles was to preach to these tribes wherever they were, world-wide. (The decision to include non-Jews, the Gentiles, came later (see page 16), but that was also on a world-wide basis, and probably resulted in Thomas going to India. The apostles were intended to be on the move. They were eye witnesses of the great events in the Jesus story, from the beginning of his ministry to the Ascension, and they had been trained by him, while disciples, to preach the Gospel. No one else was in this special position of being able to say 'I was there, I saw these things with my own eyes, and am telling you what Jesus told me!' In old age they may have settled down, too old to travel, so the tradition that St Peter became the leader of the Church in Rome does not conflict with his role as a travelling preacher.

In places where their preaching was successful and Christian communities were established, the apostles appointed men to lead them. In Acts it says, 'They also appointed elders for them in each congregation, and with prayer and fasting committed them to the Lord in whom they had put their faith' (Acts 14:23). These were to be men of high moral character as well as devout Christians. St Paul wrote a letter to Timothy, one of his missionary companions, whom he had left in a city called Ephesus with the task of organising and helping the local Christian churches. In the letter he told him what kind of men to choose as leaders:

> Our leader [the Greek word is *presbyteros*], therefore, or bishop, must be above reproach, faithful to his one wife, sober, temperate, courteous, hospitable, and a good teacher; he must not be given to drink, or a brawler, but of a forbearing disposition, avoiding quarrels, and no lover of money. He must be one who manages his own household well and wins obedience from his children, and a man of the highest principles. If a man does not know how to control his own family, how can he look after a congregation of God's people? He must not be a convert newly baptized, for fear the sin of conceit should bring upon him a judgement contrived by the devil. He must moreover have a good reputation with the non-Christian public, so that he may not be exposed to scandal and get caught in the devil's snare.

> Deacons, likewise, must be men of high principle, not indulging in double talk, given neither to excessive drinking nor to money-grubbing. They must be men who combine a clear conscience with a firm hold on the deep truths of our faith. No less than bishops, they must first undergo a scrutiny, and if there is no mark against them, they may serve. Their wives, equally, must be women of high principle, who will not talk scandal, sober and trustworthy in every way. A deacon must be faithful to his one wife, and good at managing his children and his own household. For deacons with a good record of service may claim a high standing and the right to speak openly on matters of the Christian faith.

> 1 Timothy 3:2–13

1 List the qualities of a *presbyteros*, then those of a deacon. Do they differ very much? If so how and why?

2 Discuss why St Paul thought it was so important for church leaders to have the particular qualities which he lists.

The word *presbyteros* has given Christians a lot of trouble, as has another *episcopos* which is found in Acts 20:28. (The New English Bible translates it as shepherds. Look at other versions of these verses.) The Greek words means elder and overseer. They are probably just synonyms in the New Testament. The issue at debate is what an elder or overseer did. By the third century he was responsible for a number of churches in a region and for appointing the men who looked after them directly, who came to be called priests. He and the priests were now specially consecrated men who alone were allowed to celebrate the sacrament of the Eucharist. Was this one of their functions in the church of New Testament times? Members of the Roman Catholic, Orthodox and Anglican denominations would say that it was.

Bishops

A bishop is in charge of a diocese, that is a geographical area, which might cover the Indian Ocean or New York. He is a priest who has been appointed to a greater supervisory role. He also ordains priests, and carries out confirmation ceremonies.

Priests

The principal function of a priest is to administer the sacraments, but they usually have pastoral (that is, counselling and helping) and administrative roles as well. Parson, vicar, or rector is the name which is given to priests who are responsible for parishes. A parish is a geographical area, the smallest part of a diocese.

Deacons

In Acts 6 as well as in the passage from 1 Timothy, deacons are mentioned. Their duty was to serve the church so that the apostles and elders or overseers could be freed for their spiritual ministry. Nowadays, there are two kinds of deacon in the Anglican churches and some others. One is a man who intends to become a priest. After one year as a deacon he will be ordained into the priesthood. The second is a man or woman who acts as an assistant clergy person. Such a deacon will visit the sick, teach and preach at services. He or she can baptise, take marriages and conduct funeral services. They may assist at a Eucharist, but no deacon of any kind may consecrate the elements of bread and wine. Only priests can do this.

A priest offering the sign of peace to some members of his congregation. Can you suggest what role the two women whose heads are covered have in the Church?

Cardinals

In the Roman Catholic Church, for the last 800 years or more, popes have appointed men to advise them and help them administer the world-wide Church. These men, who are usually bishops, are called cardinals. On the death of a pope they elect his successor, normally from among themselves.

Patriarch

This is a title which means father or head of a family or tribe. It is applied to the leaders of the churches which make up the Orthodox Church.

Laity

The vast majority of Christians are not ordained. They constitute the people of God, the laity. This word comes from the Greek *laos*, meaning people. Some denominations do not use the word because it seems to suggest that there is a distinction between ministers and church members which they do not accept.

Protestant Churches

Each Protestant denomination evolved its own form of church government, basing it on its understanding of the clues which the New Testament provided. Generally speaking they rejected the kind of priesthood with which they were familiar in the Roman Church of their day. They claimed that the New Testament referred to Jesus as priest but in a unique way, as the one who offered himself in sacrifice, once for all. The Eucharist was not a sacrifice. The New Testament might speak of Christian elders, even bishops, and deacons but not priests. The concept of the Christian priest was alien to the Bible and came from the religions of the Roman Empire. Some Protestant denominations have bishops; they are to be found among Methodists in the USA, but not in the UK, for example. However, the most important spiritual leader in Protestant churches tends to be the minister. As the word suggests, his or her function is to minister to the local congregation. Though some Protestant Churches only ordain men, many of them also have women ministers who may hold the same offices and perform the same functions as men (see page 77).

The minister tends to be a person who acts on behalf of the people or congregation. He, or she, is set apart to perform pastoral duties and conduct services because of his or her training and spiritual suitability. The congregation agrees that this is their vocation or calling. Ordination is public recognition of this, and signifies the view of the denomination that they are fit people to perform these functions. It confers nothing in the form of spiritual power. Such Christians tend to believe in the 'gathered church'. It is there that authority lies. The ministers act on its behalf and receive their authority from it. When they use the phrase 'apostolic succession', they do not think of an unbroken line of men stretching from the apostles to the present Pope, Patriarch of Constantinople, or the Archbishop of Cape Town, for example. They are concerned about the teaching which the apostles received from Jesus and passed on. This is the 'apostolic succession' which matters to them. They believe that it is preserved in the New Testament. For that reason Protestant churches speak of the authority of scripture, not the authority of the Pope or the Church, and put their trust in it.

All the churches share certain concerns about their priests or ministers. They should be people of spirituality, morality, and learning, for their work combines that of social worker, teacher, and preacher, as well as administrator of sacraments.

Church hierarchies

The table below shows the very different hierarchies of the Roman Catholic and Presbyterian Churches, to take just two churches as an example:

Roman Catholic	Presbyterian
Pope	General Assembly
Cardinals	Presbytery Synod
Priests	Kirk session
Deacons	Local congregation of minister and elders elected
Laity	by the church members

Both denominations have a hierarchical organisation, but the Roman Catholic emphasis is on the clergy, the Presbyterian is on the minister and congregation together. The Orthodox and Anglican Churches are organised in a similar way to the Roman Catholic; the Baptist and United Reformed Churches are nearer to the Presbyterian model, though Baptists and Congregationalists emphasise the independence of each congregation.

PRAYER

It is impossible to limit the ways in which God's grace is given to human beings to the actions performed by certain people, and to the sacraments, whether they be seven or two. Christians, or some of them, are very aware of other activities through which grace is received. The commonest is probably prayer. If it is seen as a means of grace it might be understood more maturely than it sometimes is. Often Christians speak about saying their prayers and this can give the impression of telling God your troubles and leaving him to get on with the task of solving them. God's grace certainly did not take away Paul's bodily pain or danger and eventual execution (II Corinthians 12:7), any more than it gave Jesus an easy life. It gave both of them the *strength* to transcend fear and suffering.

PILGRIMAGES

Christians may regard certain places as special, such as buildings or even countries, where the presence of God can be felt. Some speak of the land of Jesus' birth as the Holy Land. When they visit the Church of the Nativity in Bethlehem, or the Church of the Holy Sepulchre, built on the site of his tomb, they are not going as tourists; they hope to find the visit sacramental, a means of receiving grace. Such a journey made in the hope of spiritual benefit is called a pilgrimage.

Lourdes

Not all pilgrimages are to Israel or to Rome, hallowed by the deaths of St Peter and St Paul. Thousands of pilgrims travel each year to a village in France called Lourdes. There in the nineteenth century a young woman, Bernadette, received a number of visions of the Virgin Mary, the mother of Jesus. Her presence has given the place qualities which might be described as sacramental. Christians, especially Roman Catholics, go there in the hope of receiving grace. Sometimes it takes the form of healing.

Pilgrims holding a service at the grotto where Bernadette received her visions. Do Roman Catholics from your district go to Lourdes?

In most of the United Kingdom holy wells are remembered only in place names such as Bridewell (St Brigit's Well) or road names, such as Holy Well Lane, but in the Irish Republic, and many other countries, they are still cared for and used. They are associated with the saints of long ago, such as St Patrick (see page 22) or St Brigit, whose parents were baptised by St Patrick and who founded the first nunnery in Ireland. These wells are renowned for such qualities as the purity of the water, their reliability even in times of drought, and their healing properties, especially of skin complaints.

A centre of pilgrimage in Wales was the shrine of St David, in the cathedral of St Davids. It is still possible to trace some of the routes taken by pilgrims and to go to some of the other sites which they would have visited. A pilgrimage could involve effort, walking for miles over rough paths. Pilgrims wanted to make the most of it and go to as many holy places as possible.

1   Look for places in your locality where pilgrimages did, or do, take place. Who made such pilgrimages, and why? Where did they come from? If they are centres of pilgrimage now try to invite a pilgrim to school to talk about the experience.

2   Invite a modern pilgrim who has been on a pilgrimage to another country to tell you about it. Perhaps you could make a log of their journey from checking in at the airport to arriving back home. Remember that it is the spiritual journey that really matters.

3   Discover some place names linked with holy wells on a map. Try to find where they were on the ground and if anything remains of them today. Discover who they were associated with and why. You may come across other places of religious significance, such as Paulsgrove (see page 21). What can you find out about them?

Warning So many new roads are being made now that naming them is becoming a problem. Well Close or St Andrew's Avenue, built in 1965, may not have the remotest link with the religious history of the district.

SAINTS

Saints have already been mentioned on pages 21–4. In the New Testament, a saint was anyone who had been sanctified by the Holy Spirit. When Paul wrote to the saints at Rome, Corinth, or Ephesus, he was simply meaning the Christians who lived there. As time passed 'saint' came to have a special meaning. It was used of the apostles and Mary, Jesus' mother, but also men and women who had proved to be great Christians, taking the Gospel into new areas, like St Patrick, St Ninian, or St David. Christians like Catherine, who was tortured on a wheel and then beheaded, or Wenceslas, king of Bohemia, who was murdered, both martyrs of the faith, also came to be called saints. Saints are prayed to by some Christians because the quality of their lives was rewarded by God who placed them close to him in heaven. They are therefore able to mediate grace to those who seek their help.

The shrines of saints are believed to have the same qualities by those who venerate them. Their earthly remains, or relics, give holiness to a place and this is communicated to people who visit them.

ICONS

The picture opposite is an icon of St Alexei. An icon is not just a picture which reminds someone of a figure (a saint) from the past. It is a means of grace – the person portrayed had great spiritual power and lives in the presence of God, the source of such power. Through the icon it becomes available to the worshipper helping her or him to be a Christian. When the icon is kissed grace is received. Its presence in the room or church is also a source of such grace, whether it is

kissed or not. Those who make icons are anonymous. No one should be able to say who made a particular icon. It bears no signature or special mark by which the artist may be identified. That is to ensure that it is the saint alone who receives honour. Icon makers must also fast, pray, and live good moral lives, for they are mediums through whom grace becomes manifest, just as much as the clergy are. Icons are normally found in an Orthodox church.

You have learned enough already for you to realise that not all Christians believe that grace may be received by using icons, going on pilgrimages, and other practices mentioned in this chapter. All Christians value prayer, and the vast majority celebrate the sacraments of Baptism and the Eucharist. However, the Society of Friends (see pages 31 and 43) and the Salvation Army (see page 32) are examples of two denominations which observe no sacraments at all.

1 Write notes on the words respect, reverence, venerate, and worship. Discuss the differences in meaning of these words.
2 Write notes on the meanings of the words holy and sacred.
3 Discuss the reasons why a Christian might find it helpful to confess sins to a priest. List the most important ones.

Chapter 8

Christian Festivals

Many religions think of certain *times* as being sacred and means of grace, as well as places, people and objects. They use festivals to celebrate these sacred times. This idea is not very strong in Christianity where the emphasis is upon using a festival to remember, give thanks, and celebrate – rather like a birthday. However, when country people in England used to believe that at Christmas animals were given the power of speech and that like humans they knelt and worshipped the infant Jesus (as it was supposed they had done in Bethlehem 2000 years before), they had something of this idea of sacred time at the back of their minds. It is present also in the thoughts of Christians entering an Orthodox Church at midnight on Easter Day, passing from the darkness outside to the brightness within, which they create with their candles. Many who sing carols and hymns on Christmas day make a journey in time as well as space from the place where they are to Bethlehem 2000 years ago.

SUNDAY

Sunday is the most sacred day of the week for Christians. It was the first day of the Jewish week – the first day of creation (Genesis 1:1–5), the day the apostles received the Holy Spirit (Acts 2) and the day Jesus rose from the dead.

In New Testament times the days of the Jewish week were numbered one to six, with the seventh day (known as the Sabbath) being kept by Jews as special. The early Christians met daily for worship (Acts 2), but gradually the Lord's Day, the *first* day of the week, became more important. For many years they kept both the Sabbath and the Lord's Day.

As the Church grew further away from its Jewish roots, the first day became a new Sabbath for Christians. In the Roman world this day of the week was the one on which the sun was honoured, thus Sunday is the name given to it in the English-speaking countries. Only when the Emperor Constantine made Christianity a legal religion did it become a day of rest. In 321 CE he forbade those who lived in towns to work on Sundays. Slaves as well as free people were included in the edict.

THE CHRISTIAN YEAR

Two dates determine when the special occasions and festivals fall. The first is the fixed date of Christmas. The second is Easter, which is called a moveable feast. It is related to the full moon after the spring equinox and can vary by over a month, from 21 March to 25 April. It is not the dates that matter most, however, but the meaning and purpose of the celebrations. In old calendars they were printed in red and so are still sometimes called red letter days. The most important, using Gregorian dating, are:

Month	Festival or season
November/December	Advent
December	Christmas (25)
	Feast of Holy Innocents (28)
January	Epiphany (6)
February	Candlemas (2)
February/March	Lent (Shrove Tuesday, Ash Wednesday, Holy Week)
March/April	Easter (Holy Week, Easter Day)
May/June	Ascension Day (Thursday after the fourth Sunday after Easter)
	Pentecost or Whitsuntide (seven Sundays after Easter)
	Trinity Sunday (Sunday after Pentecost)
	Corpus Christi (Thursday after Trinity Sunday)
	Sacred Heart of Jesus (Friday of the third week after Pentecost)

Note: The Gregorian calendar is used in most of the world. Orthodox Churches, however, still use the Julian calendar – they celebrate Christmas, for example, on 6/7 January according to the Gregorian calendar.

Advent

The Christian year begins with Advent in November. Advent means coming. Four Sundays before Christmas Christians begin to prepare to welcome the birth of Jesus. In some homes there may be Advent calendars which are opened day by day, building up the excitement and preparation for Christmas. There may be Advent candles lit in churches. The Orthodox Church prepares with a 40-day period of penitence.

Christmas

We do not know the exact year or month of Jesus' birth. We first hear of Christmas being celebrated on 25 December in the year 336 CE by Christians in Rome, roughly 300 years after Jesus' death. Twenty-fifth December was also the date which worshippers of Mithras (a Persian god in the Roman world) celebrated as his birthday. They called it *Natalis Solis Invicti* (Birthday of the Unconquered Sun).

Romans also held a festival in honour of the god Saturn on 17 December when presents were given and slaves were allowed to join in the fun. The Saturnalia, as it was called, was a time when the normal order of things was turned upside down, masters feasted their slaves who dressed in fine clothes. In the northern hemisphere it was also the time of winter solstice ceremonies to ensure that the sun would triumph over the darkness and cold which was gripping the earth. Christmas is probably a Christianising of all these events, focusing them on Jesus, the Sun of Righteousness and Light of the World. Many Christmas customs can probably be traced to these non-Christian celebrations.

The message of Christmas is that God sent his only son into the world with a message of light and love. In John's Gospel it says that Jesus was the light of the world (John 8:12) and in many stories in the New Testament he is shown to enlighten the mind with his wisdom, or overcome evil with his love. The hymns and carols of Christmas often have the themes of light and love in them. For example:

Silent night, holy night
All is calm, all is bright,
Round yon virgin mother, and child,
Holy infant so tender and mild,
Sleep in heavenly peace, sleep in heavenly peace.

Love came down at Christmas
Love all lovely, Love divine,
Love was born at Christmas,
Star and angels gave the sign.

1   Make a collection of carols and hymns which have light and love as their themes.
2   Try to decide which are carols and which are hymns. This is not easy with modern compositions. Really a carol is a joyful song which accompanies a dance. A hymn is a sacred poem set to music, usually rather solemn compared with a carol. Some Christians did not like carols to be sung in church. They were thought not to be religious enough, but now most people do not seem to mind.

Christmas customs

These vary from country to country, but because Christianity was taken by European colonisers in the eighteenth and nineteenth centuries, the customs world-wide are largely those of Europe. So, for example, it is possible to find Christmas trees and Father Christmas in India, and buy cards with snow scenes on them in lands where snow has never been seen.

The Christmas tree is pre-Christian. It is evergreen and symbolises the belief that life will survive even the cold, darkness, and apparent death of the earth which is part of a north European winter. Holly and ivy may have the same meaning. The lights on the tree may have come from ancient festivals of light. Perhaps the Jewish festival of

A Christmas crib made by members of the Cree Indian tribe of North America.

Hannukah had an influence (it falls in December and is a festival of light). Jewish Christians might have linked their festival with the birth of Jesus when Christmas began to be celebrated.

Some customs are Christian. One is the crib which is set up in churches and some homes, showing Jesus being born in a stable, though it was probably a cave, not a shed. St Nicholas, Father Christmas or Santa Claus is said to have been a bishop of Myra in modern Turkey. That explains his robes which are something like the vestments of a bishop. He is said to have heard that three sisters were unable to marry because their father could not afford their dowries, so he left three bags of gold secretly at their home. This may be the reason for giving presents, but it was something that also happened at the Saturnalia, as was the custom of having a feast.

1 List as many Christmas customs as you can. You may be able to find out about customs in a number of different countries from people who have travelled and lived in them.
2 Try to discover what Christian symbolism has become attached to them, as the ideas of light, life, and hope, are linked with the tree.

Feast of the Holy Innocents

When he heard that a 'king' had been born in Bethlehem, the ruler of Judea, Herod the Great, ordered all male children under two years of age to be killed. The tragedy is commemorated at this time to remind Christians that suffering is part of life, as well as enjoyment, and of the innocent Jesus who died on the cross. Christians who celebrate this festival do so by holding a special Eucharist or Mass.

Epiphany

This is a Greek word which means manifestation. It is usually taken as referring to Jesus being shown to the wise men by his mother. In the Gospels there are very few stories of Jesus preaching to Gentiles. His mission seems to have been to the Jews. As we have already noticed, it was some time before the apostles agreed that non-Jews could become Christians. This story of 'wise men from the east' (no one knows how many, except artists who always show three!) is therefore very important because it tells of God guiding them to his son, the light of the world. It is taken by Christians to mean that God intended everyone to be brought to Jesus. The account is in Matthew 2. No one knows who the wise men actually were. Some bibles use the word magi, which is a direct translation of the Greek, others call them astrologers. You might like to find out what other words are used.

In Britain people some times refer to the twelve days of Christmas. Epiphany is the last of these and may be marked in the home by taking down decorations. In the eastern churches, Epiphany still commemorates three manifestations, the birth, baptism, and Jesus' first miracle at the wedding at Cana (John 2:1–11). Christians who celebrate Epiphany do so by holding a special Eucharist or Mass.

Candlemas

This is a very old festival which is known by several names, including the Purification of the Blessed Virgin Mary and the Presentation of Christ in the Temple. Candlemas is the Old English name. Lighted candles were carried in procession in churches and gave cheer in the winter gloom before there was electric lighting. The celebration commemorates the presentation of Jesus in the Temple 40 days after his birth (Luke 2:22–35). On seeing him an old man called Simeon spoke some beautiful and famous words which are used in many Christian services:

> Lord, now let your servant go in peace:
> Your word has been fulfilled.
> My own eyes have seen the salvation:
> Which you have prepared in the sight of every people;
> A light to reveal you to the nations:
> And the glory of your people Israel.

> Alternative Service Book

The Roman Catholic Church still celebrates this festival with a procession of candles.

Easter

Lent
Shrove Tuesday   The Easter cycle begins with Shrove Tuesday in practice. This is the last day before Lent, which is a time of fasting. All rich foods and the ingredients for making them should be removed from the house so that no one might be tempted to break the fast.

What better way to do this than to have a feast! These celebrations are known by two names, Mardi Gras and Carnival. Some people will be surprised to find either of these linked with Shrove Tuesday. August tends to be the time for carnivals in Britain and other north European countries, and few whenever they are held seem to have much to do with religion. Yet carnival means farewell to meat, *carnem levare* in Latin. Mardi Gras is 'fat Tuesday'. Carnival could be a long feast lasting for months, beginning any time after Epiphany. It is still three days long in Rio de Janeiro, in Brazil.

In the UK on Shrove Tuesday fat is used up in pancakes and in some places egg races are held. The climate does not really lend itself to street parties in February or March, and British religion tends to be rather sober and restrained.

Shrove Tuesday actually takes its name from the practice of being shriven, that is of going to confession and receiving absolution for the sins which had been committed, so that Lent could be entered in a state of purity.

Ash Wednesday   Lent proper starts on Ash Wednesday. In some churches the palm crosses kept from Palm Sunday the year before are burnt and the ash, in the sign of the cross, put on the forehead of the penitent. In the Bible there are many references to people who had done wrong dressing in sackcloth and ashes to show that they repented. Lent is a 40-day fast but actually the period is a little longer because Sundays are not included among the fast days.

Mothering Sunday   This is the fourth Sunday in Lent. Sundays in Lent are feast days not fast days, so enjoyment is permitted. Mothering Sunday should be one of the happiest days of all. It is a time when Christians, and many other people, show their appreciation of all that their mothers have done for them by giving them cards, presents and, especially, flowers. In church children are often given little posies of violets to take to their mothers. The flowers may be blessed by special prayers being said by the minister or priest who then gives them to children, and sometimes adults who come to him, or her, to receive them. This festival is a revival of a past custom of visiting the mother church of the district, the cathedral. The traditional reading for the day was from the Letter to the Galatians 4 which includes the words, 'Jerusalem . . . our mother'.

Holy Week   This is the period from Palm Sunday to Easter Day. It commemorates the last week in Jesus' life. It is during these days that preparations for Easter reach their climax.

In some countries public processions and other activities remind everyone, whether they are Christian or not, of the death of Jesus. In Seville, a Spanish city, confraternities (associations for people living in particular districts or working together, in the tobacco factory for example) walk together in processions which converge on the

A Holy Week (Semana Santa) *procession in Seville.*

cathedral. The penitents wear masks for the intention is not to draw attention to themselves but to the sufferings of Jesus. On Holy Wednesday, the pain of Jesus and of his mother, Mary, who watched him being led to his execution, is remembered. On Holy Thursday aspects of the processions remind onlookers of the Last Supper and arrest. The penitents walk to the cathedral bare-footed on Holy Friday, *Viernes Santo*, to experience something of the pain of Jesus. Already the road surface may be blisteringly hot, in contrast to the cold of the marble floors of the cathedral. In some countries penitents may whip themselves, imitating the flagellation which Jesus had to endure.

Customs vary and keep changing. In the UK processions in Holy Week tend to happen only on Good Friday, and are recent developments or revivals or old traditions. They are often used as opportunities for Christians of different denominations to show that the Cross unites them in one faith, as well as reminding the population at large of the Easter message. In medieval times passion plays were sometimes performed, telling the story of Jesus' betrayal, arrest, death and resurrection.

The main events of Holy Week in the UK are the giving of palm crosses to members of the congregation on Palm Sunday, especially in the Anglican and Roman Catholic Churches, the Queen's gift of money to selected elderly men and women on Maundy Thursday, and the services on Good Friday.

Palm Sunday Like Mothering Sunday, Palm Sunday brings a pleasant break in the rather grim journey towards Easter for those who observe Lent. It is the day when Christians remember Jesus' entry into Jerusalem to the cheers of the crowds who took down branches from the nearby palm trees and threw them in his path as a sign of honour and welcome.

In countries where palm trees grow outdoors as a natural part of the vegetation, Christians will process through streets carrying palm branches in their hands. In the UK worshippers may be given a cross made from a palm leaf. They are likely to keep it at home until the next year, perhaps hanging it on a wall in one of the rooms. Special hymns and readings from the Bible which describe Jesus' Palm Sunday ride will remind any worshipper or visitor of the anniversary which is being celebrated.

Maundy Thursday   The main event of this day in the last week of Jesus' ministry was the Last Supper. During the meal he took a bowl of water and a towel and washed his disciples' feet to teach them humility. After doing it he said, 'I have set you an example: you are to do as I have done for you. In very truth I tell you, a servant is not greater than his master, nor a messenger than the one who sent him. If you know this, happy are you if you act upon it' (John 13:15–17).

Popes and princes have often followed Jesus' example by washing the feet of beggars or old people. In the UK, the Queen takes part in a Maundy service which is held in a different cathedral each year and gives special Maundy money, contained in a purse, to local old people.

Queen Elizabeth II presenting purses of Maundy money at Chichester Cathedral in 1986. The number of people who receive them matches the monarch's age.

Good Friday   This is the most solemn day in the Christian year. Everyone remembers the death of Jesus and special services are held, especially between 12 noon and 3 p.m., the time when Jesus actually hung on the cross and died. Roman Catholic, Orthodox and Anglican churches are likely to look very austere compared with their usual appearance. There will be no floral decorations or anything else to take attention away from the cross or crucifix. The hot cross-bun is a popular way of remembering the crucifixion at home. The old custom of eating fish on a Friday, which is not often observed in England now, is kept in quite a number of homes on this particular Friday.

Easter Day

The Saturday of Easter week has no special ceremonies associated with it. It has become a popular time for weddings because of the long holiday weekend, breaking a tradition that no weddings were held during Lent. Late in the evening, shortly before midnight Orthodox Christians will gather outside the church door in the darkness. They are like the mourners who went to the tomb of Jesus. Then, at midnight, the doors are flung wide open and the congregation flood into the brightly lit church to celebrate the Resurrection. In some churches the church may remain in darkness, and the congregation enters carrying candles which they light and use to search for the body of Jesus. Then the cry goes up, 'Christ is risen.' Everyone replies, 'He is risen indeed.'

In many other churches the Easter celebrations begin with a Eucharist at the normal time, but it may be accompanied by an extra peal of bells and the inside of the church will be decked with flowers. The gloom of the previous few days has gone; the hymns express joy and gratitude. Women especially are likely to dress in bright clothes to match the occasion, and some people will use Easter as an excuse to buy new ones.

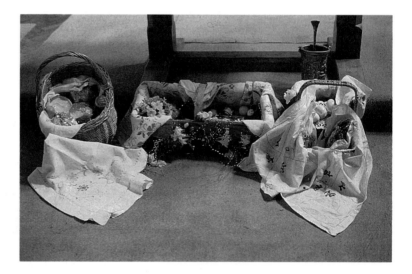

Eggs and bread for blessing on Holy Saturday (an east European custom). What symbolic links do they have with Easter?

Eggs feature in the Easter customs of many countries. The most well-known in the UK is the giving of chocolate eggs, but elsewhere there are customs involving painted eggs, hard-boiled eggs and hidden eggs. Find out about some of these customs and the reasons for them. Suggest as many reasons as you can for the significance of eggs at Easter.

For most people Easter ends on the Sunday, Easter Day, though in some countries the following Monday is a public holiday. However, churches celebrate Easter for 50 days, until Pentecost.

Ascension Day

This is the one important event to be remembered in this period. Forty days after Easter, always on a Thursday, Christians mark the end of Jesus' earthly ministry with services which remind them of his return to the Father. It is rarely a public holiday and often passes unnoticed. Not all churches have special services. Many will remember the occasion on the following Sunday.

Pentecost

Even though the Church year begins in Advent, this festival is often called the birthday of the Church. Fifty days after Easter the disciples were celebrating the festival of *Shavuot* with their fellow Jews. *Pentecost* is the Greek name for it, and simply means 50. They were thanking God for giving them the Torah, the five books of Moses on Mount Sinai, for that is the purpose of *Shavuot*. They experienced the presence and power of God within them in a new way, but one which Jesus had warned them to expect and which the prophets had spoken about. It had been a rare gift in the past but Joel had said that one day it would be 'poured out on all humankind' (Joel 2:28–9). It was the event the disciples had been waiting for before starting out on their own preaching mission. Jesus had said, 'I am sending upon you my Father's promised gift; so stay here in this city until you are armed with power from above' (Luke 24:49).

Sometimes the day is called Whitsunday because new members of the church were often baptised at this time and wore white to signify a new beginning to their lives. 'Whit walks', processions by Christians of several churches in a district, were a common feature of Whit Monday, the day after Pentecost, especially in the north of England. They were accompanied by bands from the Salvation Army, Scouts or Boys' Brigade. Picnics and sporting events followed. Some of these still happen. The origins, however, seem to have been the village club, a kind of insurance association, rather than Christian. Surplus funds were spent on entertainment. You might be able to find out from some older people what happened at 'Whit' when they were young. Discover what takes place today, and try to explain the changes.

Discuss the arguments Christians might put forward for keeping or changing the dates of Easter and Pentecost. (Until a few years ago Whitsuntide was a public holiday in the UK. Now the Spring Bank Holiday has replaced it and is fixed at the end of May.)

Trinity Sunday

The Sunday after Pentecost is set aside for remembering the Christian doctrine of God as Father, Son and Holy Spirit. A famous hymn sung at this time begins:

> Holy, holy, holy, Lord God all mighty,
> Early in the morning our songs shall rise to thee,
> Holy, holy, holy, merciful and mighty,
> God in three persons blessed Trinity.

James Montgomery

Priests are often ordained on this day in the western churches. In the eastern churches the Festival of All Saints is celebrated on this Sunday. The western tradition is to keep All Saints on 1 November.

Corpus Christi

This is the Latin form of the phrase, 'the body of Christ' which is spoken at the Eucharist. In Roman Catholic churches there is a daily celebration of the Eucharist or Mass, but in 1264 it was decided to honour the Mass with a special celebration which should take place on the Thursday after Trinity Sunday. Originally Maundy Thursday was the day dedicated to giving thanks for the Eucharist, but it did not seem proper to rejoice during Holy Week and especially on the day when Jesus was betrayed, so the festival was moved. After the Mass the host (the consecrated bread) is placed in a special container called a monstrance and carried in procession. The

monstrance has a glass window in the centre so that the host can be seen. That is why it is called a monstrance. The word is similar to demonstrate, which means to show. Catholic villages in continental Europe are often beautifully prepared for the Corpus Christi procession to pass through the streets. Leaves from trees and the petals of flowers are laid on the pavements and roads as decorations. Sometimes they depict scenes from the Gospels. Nothing like this occurs in the UK except at Arundel in Sussex. In the Roman Catholic cathedral a carpet of flowers (see left) is laid in the main aisle of the nave, from the door to the steps leading to the high altar.

The Sacred Heart of Jesus

This is held on the Friday of the third week after Pentecost. It is celebrated only by Roman Catholics and was included in the calendar as recently as 1856. Its purpose is to encourage devotion to the heart of Jesus, a symbol of his love, compassion, and suffering.

<table>
<tr><td>

Chapter

9

</td><td>

Mary, the Mother of Jesus

</td></tr>
</table>

Jesus' mother, Mary, is very highly venerated in the Roman Catholic and Orthodox Churches, but less so among Protestant Christians.

In the New Testament she obviously plays an important part in the birth stories of Jesus (Matthew 1–2; Luke 1–2). However, these accounts do not simply mention her role as mother, they also refer to her obedience to God's will. She is naturally alarmed not only to receive an angelic visitation, but also to learn that she, a virgin, is about to conceive (Luke 1:26–36). The episode ends, however, with Mary composing a beautiful hymn of praise, which is used in the worship of many denominations. It is usually called the *Magnificat*, from its first words in the Latin version. It begins:

> Tell out my soul the greatness of the Lord,
> rejoice, rejoice, my spirit, in God my saviour;
>
> Luke 1:46-7

The story brings out her obedience, humility, and innocence – qualities of character which painters and writers have emphasised ever since.

Mary is usually only a background figure during Jesus' ministry. Sometimes he appears rather casual in his attitude to her. At the wedding at Cana (see page 8) she tells him that the wine has run out, and he replies, 'Mother, your concern is not mine'; but then Mary tells the servants to do whatever he says, as though she knew that his answer was not his last word (John 2:1–7). There is also an occasion when Jesus' mother and brothers wanted to speak to him and he replied to the man who brought the message that they were waiting, 'Who is my mother? Who are my brothers? ... Whoever does the will of my heavenly Father is my brother, my sister, my mother (Matthew 12:48–50; see also Mark 3:31–5). Mary is at the foot of the cross when Jesus is crucified (John 19:25) and with the disciples after the Ascension (Acts 1:14), but that is the last mention of her in the Bible.

The Roman and Orthodox Churches have shown steadily increasing veneration for Mary since the fifth century. The Council of Ephesus in 431 CE, an assembly of the most important church leaders of the time, gave her the title *Theotokos*, God-bearer, which upset some Christians, though it was correct in a way if Jesus was God. Some would have preferred *Christotokos*, Christ-bearer. The belief also

A Marian holy well in Ireland

developed that Mary, like Elijah (the Hebrew prophet) and Jesus, was taken bodily into heaven at the end of her life. This can be traced back to the sixth century but the Roman Catholic Church only officially defined the doctrine in 1950, saying that the Blessed Virgin Mary, 'having completed her earthly life, was in body and soul assumed into heavenly glory'. Another doctrine, that of the Immaculate Conception of the Virgin Mary, was the subject of considerable argument in the Middle Ages. It was generally accepted by Roman Catholics in the sixteenth century and defined as a dogma (the official teaching or doctrine of the Church) in 1854. It declares that, 'from the very moment of her conception the Blessed Virgin Mary was . . . kept free from all stain of original sin'.

The Roman Catholic and Orthodox Churches, and other Christians who venerate Mary, are eager to say that she was no ordinary woman, but someone very special: the one chosen by God to be the mother of his Son. Protestant Christians tend to say that this veneration verges on worship, and that the uniqueness of Jesus is threatened by suggestions that Mary and the saints should be objects of devotion and people who can mediate God's grace. They also fail to find these doctrines in the Bible, their source of authority, and therefore refuse to accept them.

1   Discuss the views that different Christians have of the Virgin Mary.
2   Write down as many reasons as you can for
   a) venerating her
   b) not venerating her.

FEASTS OF THE BLESSED VIRGIN MARY

The special feasts of the Blessed Virgin Mary are:
- The Nativity of the Blessed Virgin Mary – 8 September
- The Immaculate Conception of the Blessed Virgin Mary – 8 December
- The Annunciation of the Lord – 25 March
- The Assumption of the Blessed Virgin Mary – 15 August
- The Solemnity of Mary, Mother of God – 1 January. This celebrates the coronation of Mary in heaven.

The Feast of the Assumption in a Corfu Village

Fran Morley, a Roman Catholic, wrote this account of the Feast of the Assumption which she witnessed while on holiday in Corfu.

The tiny village of Hlomos lies south of Messongi on the eastern side of Corfu. The community is Greek Orthodox and religion, with its elaborate ceremonies, is taken very seriously. The Feast of the Assumption is a particular favourite and often celebrated with feasting and dancing as we had witnessed on the island of Crete a couple of years before. In Hlomos we shared in a rather different celebration.

The little church was on the outskirts of the village and we found the streets almost empty as the people had already gathered around it for the service. I say 'around' advisedly because the church was too small for more than a few people to be inside it at one time. As we arrived we met a boatman we had seen before, and he immediately directed the men in our group to one side of the building and the women to the other! Apparently the sexes were segregated for worship. The interior of the church could only be glimpsed through a garlanded north door outside which a crowd of older women had gathered to follow the service. The singing of the priest rose and fell in a chant from which we recognised some phrases. *Kyrie Eleison*, Lord have mercy,was one of them [Greek words such as these are sometimes used by Roman Catholics, which explains how Fran recognised them]. By standing on tiptoe we could see the candles burning and the bearded face of the young priest framed in the central arch of the screen which hid the sanctuary.

It was a social as well as religious gathering. Small children played in the shade of olive trees and cedars, donkeys chewed the thistles, young people in their feast-day best eyed one another covertly. The collection plate was followed by several large baskets of bread rolls which were distributed among us. The bread was sweet and tasted of honey. Someone began to ring the bells and small boys queued up to have a turn. One, under-standably, had his fingers in his ears. The noise was tremendous! Inside the church people were receiving Holy Communion. First, though, each person went to an icon of the Virgin Mary near the font. They crossed themselves, kissed the picture, and indicated that we should do the same. Only then could we join the queue for Communion. The wine was offered by the priest on a curved spoon. We helped ourselves to small squares of blessed bread from a basket.

Afterwards, we were taken to another little church with a cemetery around it. A man brought feast-day bread to his mother's grave. She had been buried only three days before and he wore the old symbol of mourning, a black crepe armband. He broke the bread and shared it with us. There was a simplicity and sincerity about everything that was quite timeless.

During the Feast of the Assumption on the Greek island of Tinos, some women crawl to church on their hands and knees as a sign of humility and repentence.

THE ROSARY

The Virgin Mary is remembered very specially by Roman Catholic Christians who use a rosary to help them when they pray. A rosary is a string of beads made up of five groups of ten beads with a bead (often larger) dividing each group. The groups of beads are called decades. A crucifix with five more beads hangs from the rosary.

The purpose of the rosary is to help a person remember the 15 great mysteries of the catholic faith. These are divided into three groups:

- *The Five Joyful Mysteries*
    1   The Annunciation when Mary is told that she is to be the mother of Jesus (Luke 1:26)
    2   The Visitation of Mary to her cousin Elizabeth (Luke 1:39–45)
    3   The Nativity, or birth, of Jesus
    4   The presentation of Jesus in the Temple (Luke 2:21–35)
    5   Finding Jesus in the Temple when he was taken to Jerusalem at the age of twelve and went missing. His parents found him in the Temple (Luke 2:42–50)
- *The Five Sorrowful Mysteries*
    1   Jesus' agony in the Garden of Gethsemane just before his arrest when he prayed that the cup of suffering might be taken from him (Luke 22:39–45)
    2   The scourging of Jesus (Mark 15:6–15)
    3   The crowning with thorns (Matthew 27:28–9)
    4   The way of the cross (Luke 23:25–31)
    5   The Crucifixion (John 19:16–22)
- *The Five Glorious Mysteries*
    1   The Resurrection
    2   The Ascension

3   The descent of the Holy Spirit at Pentecost
4   The Assumption of the Virgin Mary into heaven
5   The coronation of the Virgin Mary and the glory of all the saints

How the Rosary is Used

The rosary is passed through the fingers, bead by bead. Each bead acts as a reminder to the person using it.

Generally, only one set of mysteries is remembered at a time, the Five Joyful Mysteries, for example:

1   The crucifix and the five beads – the person will say the Lord's Prayer, three *Ave Marias* and a *Gloria* (each bead represents one of these)
2   The first large bead – the person will say the Lord's Prayer (each large bead represents the Lord's Prayer)
3   The first decade – the person will say an *Ave Maria* for each of the ten beads, and with each bead the person will remember the first of the Five Joyful Mysteries (The Annunciation)
4   The person will then say a *Gloria*
5   The steps 2–4 are repeated for each of the remaining Joyful Mysteries, by which time the person will have used each bead on the rosary.

The words of the *Ave Maria* (Hail Mary) are:

> Hail Mary, full of grace,
> the Lord is with you.
> Blessed are you among women
> and blessed is the fruit of your womb, Jesus.
> Holy Mary, mother of God,
> Pray for us sinners now, and at the hour of our death, Amen.

The words of the *Gloria* are:

> Glory be to the Father, and to the Son,
> and to the Holy Spirit (Ghost),
> as it was in the beginning, is now, and ever shall be,
> world without end, Amen.

?

1   Try to obtain a rosary and learn how it is used. As you hold it think how a Roman Catholic Christian can be helped by it to remember the main features of the Christian faith.
2   Discuss how using the rosary might help people in their daily lives. Write down the most important suggestions.

Chapter 10

The Ecumenical Movement

We have seen in Chapter 4 that the Christian Church had divided into many churches or denominations. Perhaps there was much diversity in it from the very beginning. In this chapter we will discuss the sense of guilt that has grown during the last hundred years – a sense of guilt because the Church is not united. In John's Gospel it says that Jesus prayed that his followers might be united. He said, 'May they all be one: as thou, Father, art in me, and I in thee, so also may they be in us, that the world may believe that thou didst send me' (John 17:21).

European missionaries found that they were preaching the Gospel in Africa or India, but then expecting the converts to become Methodists, Presbyterians, Roman Catholics, Anglicans, or members of one of the other denominations. They were asked 'Why can't we just become Christians?' or 'What is wrong with the kinds of Christianity that we already knew about?', such as the church of those whose ancestors claim to have been converted by St Thomas?

When European Christians went to India in the sixteenth century they were amazed to find that their beliefs were not unknown. They discovered that there were already Christians in India, the descendants of men and women who had been converted by St Thomas, better known as 'doubting Thomas', the disciple who at first refused to believe in the resurrection of Jesus (John 20:24–31). An Indian tradition says that after Pentecost the twelve apostles drew lots to decide where they should preach. St Thomas drew India. Long before the name of Jesus had ever been heard in most of Europe, including Britain, it was known in India. The body of St Thomas is buried in Madras Cathedral.

In India today, in cities like Bangalore or Calcutta it is possible to find ten denominations, each claiming to be the right one. No wonder some Indians or Africans refuse to take them seriously.

ATTEMPTS TO UNITE CHRISTIANS

The ecumenical movement started in 1910 with the World Missionary Conference held in Edinburgh. People still talked about winning the world for Christ in their lifetime, but they also began to discuss ways of cooperating rather than being rivals. They recognised that God was not honoured by imposing European divisions upon new converts to whom they meant nothing. An International Missionary Council was established.

In 1938 plans were laid to set up a World Council of Churches, but the Second World War led to a delay of ten years. The Council was eventually founded at Amsterdam in 1948. Its headquarters are in Geneva. Most denominations are members but the Roman Catholic Church only became deeply involved after the Second Vatican Council (1962–5).

Many countries have their own organisation through which Christians work together. In the UK it is the British Council of Churches*. At local levels there are councils of churches which may organise Good Friday walks, religious pop or gospel concerts, Christian Aid Week collections, debates between politicians at election time, the Week of Prayer for Christian Unity every January, Holy Week services and other inter-church activities.

? Try to find out whether there is a Council of Churches in your district. What does it do?

THE CHURCH AT THE CENTRE

Your parish church serving Tanhouse, Birch Green & Westbrook

A United Church of
• The Church of England
• The Methodist Church
• The Baptist Church
• The United Reformed Church

SUNDAY SERVICES
9.30 a.m. HOLY COMMUNION except on the first Sunday in the month
11.00 a.m. FAMILY SERVICE With Holy Communion on the first Sunday in the month

WEDNESDAYS
11.00 a.m. HOLY COMMUNION
Baptisms & Weddings by arrangement

TEAM MINISTRY
The Revd. Andrew Edwards
The Revd. Bob Andrews
The Revd. Derryck Evans

THE ROMAN CATHOLIC MASS
is celebrated here on Saturdays at 11.00 a.m.

The noticeboard outside Skelmersdale Ecumenical Centre, Lancashire.

If you have listed the church buildings in the area where you live (see page 33), you may have something like this:

Church of England, twelfth century (Roman church until the Reformation)
Baptist, 1750
Methodist, 1835
Roman Catholic, 1840

You might even have more than one kind of Methodist church, because that denomination divided into several groups which came together again in 1932. However, you may also have United Free Church, 1975. You will probably find that Methodists, members of the United Reformed Church and perhaps some other Christians meet together there. You might even find that a decision was taken to sell older buildings and join together.

This kind of reuniting of Christians has not happened very often. In Scotland, however, the Secession and Relief Churches came together to form the United Presbyterian Church in 1847. In 1900 they and the Free Presbyterians combined to produce the United Free Presbyterians, and in 1929 they joined the Church of Scotland in a denomination which kept that name. In 1972 the Presbyterian Church of England and the Congregational Church became the United Reformed Church. However, an attempt to unite Anglicans and Methodists in England failed.

*From August 1990 it is called the Council of Churches for Britain and Ireland. Roman Catholics are fully represented for the first time.

The most successful reunion of Christians has probably been in India. The Church of South India, inaugurated by an Act of Union in 1947, includes the Anglican Church of India, Methodists, Congregationalists, and Presbyterians. Canada is another of many countries where Christians are moving closer together. In 1925 the Methodists, Congregationalists and Presbyterians formed the United Church of Canada.

There were people who thought it possible that all Christians would become united in one Church. Now fewer of them expect this to happen. The slogan today tends to be: not union but unity. Diversity is regarded as a good thing, so long as cooperation is possible. Even if uniformity might be achieved it might not be in the best interests of Christianity.

? In your notebooks write the words unity, uniformity, diversity. Decide what each means and write a sentence giving your explanation. Then list reasons why they might be considered good *and* harmful for Christianity.

DIVISIONS BETWEEN CHRISTIANS TODAY

There are five things which divide Christians today: tradition, papal authority, baptism, priesthood, and the status of women.

Tradition

Human beings tend to prefer things to remain as they are rather than welcome drastic changes. So, although Methodists reunited in England in 1932, it was possible for a long time to find two different groups of Methodists living in the same village, each struggling to keep their buildings heated, lit and in good repair. The same village might have a Congregational church facing the same problems. Once a hundred worshippers may have gone to each church every Sunday. By 1970 there may have been fewer than ten. Natural reluctance to change and a feeling that the place where they were brought up and married, where parents and grandparents are buried, are reasons why separate churches survive at local level. In the period since 1970 more united churches have been formed because the cost of maintaining buildings, the deaths of old members, and the movement away to find work, have forced unwelcome decisions to be made.

Papal authority

The Pope still claims to be the head of the Christian Church, the successor of St Peter who was appointed by Jesus. This is something which Protestant Christians cannot accept. The Roman Catholic Church *has* become more liberal and less authoritarian; there has been more power-sharing among cardinals and bishops. The voice of the laity is listened to more than it was. However, the suspicions of

Protestant Christians remain. They would point to such things as the outspoken South American priest who was ordered to remain silent for a year as an act of penance in 1988.

Baptism

Baptism is a matter which prevents Baptists entering into full union with denominations like the United Reformed Church or Congregationalists with whom they have much in common. This is because Baptists believe that only the baptism of believers is found in the New Testament and they wish to be faithful to this principal.

Priesthood

In the Anglican Church there are members who regard the priest as a special person ordained to administer the sacraments, an exclusive role which no one else can undertake. There are other members who see him more as a minister whose other duties, of preaching, teaching and pastoral care, are as important as that of celebrating the Eucharist. In the USA there are Methodist bishops, and Protestants have accepted them in the Church of South India, so they need not be a serious obstacle.

The Status of Women

This became a major issue in 1988. On 24 September 1988 a black Anglican woman priest, the Reverend Barbara Harris, was elected bishop of Massachusetts. As a priest she had not been too much of a threat. Her activities were limited by her bishop and any bishop into whose diocese she went. He could refuse her permission to celebrate the Eucharist. Now she is a bishop that is not so easy to do. After all, she is an equal. She can also ordain priests, so it may be expected

that women who cannot be more than deacons in the UK will head for Boston. The Church of England has discussed the ordination of women for a number of years, but Bishop Harris' appointment has added urgency to the debate. There are still many Anglicans who cannot accept women as priests and bishops. They tend to hold the view, put forward by Pope John Paul in the same month that Bishop Harris was elected, that Jesus chose not to ordain women though he could have done so if he wished. His choice of men to be apostles had nothing to do with social conditioning; the Mediterranean world of the first century was male-dominated but this would not have deterred Jesus. Therefore

Bishop Barbara Harris.

it is clear that women may not be priests. In a document called *Mulieris Dignitatem* (On the Dignity of Women) the Pope wrote, 'The personal resources of the female sex are not inferior to those of the male, they are simply different.'

The Pope's statement has disappointed many Christians who do believe that the churches must respond to social change. They might point out that although Jesus chose men for his twelve closest disciples (see page 13), this does not necessarily mean that he regarded women as unfit to be his disciples. The outer circle of his disciples *did* include women. Equally he could have chosen Gentiles for his first disciples, but he did not. This did not prevent Gentiles becoming Christians (see page 16); Paul is an obvious example. Likewise, we could assume that because the disciples were all Jews, only Jewish Christians can become priests. Obviously this is not true.

However, more seriously, the Pope's statement reminds them of his power, and keeps their suspicions alive!

1   Find out whether Christians are working together in your area. What kinds of things are they doing?
2   List the reasons which are put forward by Christians for *and* against women priests. Which seem to be the most important on both sides of the argument?
(Remember, there are denominations which have women ministers but do not share the view of priesthood which is at issue here.)

Taizé

During the twentieth century a number of ecumenical communities have developed. One of these is Taizé in France. Another is Corrymeela in Northern Ireland (see page 115).

The Taizé community was founded by Roger Schutz, a Protestant born in Switzerland in 1915. As a teenager he had lived with a Roman Catholic family, and he wanted to do something to bring together the two Christian groups. He bought a house in a small village called Taizé in 1940, but the war had begun and it became a place of refuge for Jews and other people trying to escape from the Nazis. In 1942, while he was smuggling refugees into Switzerland he heard that a villager had betrayed him to the authorities so he crossed the border too and stayed in Switzerland until France was liberated in 1944. During this time he collected a group of friends around him who shared his idea of establishing a community.

Now Taizé is a place to which Christians, and sometimes young people of other faiths or of no religious beliefs, come. Over 100 000 visitors arrive each year, staying for a few days or several weeks. The small house, bought from a poor woman who needed the money, has given way to a large church, the Church of the Reconciliation, and many other buildings. Some are hostels, but people also camp.

Members of the Taizé community and visitors at prayer in the Church of the Reconciliation, Taizé.

The brothers who are members of this ecumenical monastic community have taken vows of celibacy, community of possessions, obedience to the Prior and agree to live by the Rule of the Community. At Taizé there are brothers, both Catholics and non-Catholics, from many different countries, and the community's work has spread abroad to such places as Japan, the USA, the Phillipines, Brazil and Eastern Europe.

One of the key themes of the life and meetings at Taizé is the reconciling of the apparent opposition between prayer and action, between the inner life and social involvement. Many people choose to spend a week in silence at Taizé. In 1988, Brother Roger was awarded the UNESCO peace prize, echoing Taizé's concern for sharing and justice in the world.

1   Iona is another example of an ecumenical community. Try to find Iona on a map (*clue*: it is an island off the coast of Scotland). Why was this particular island chosen? What else can you discover about the Iona Community?

2   Discuss how young Christians of different denominations might be helped by living together for a week? What kinds of things do you think they would want to talk about? Draw up a list.

   If those Christians were then to spend a week with members of other faiths what kinds of things do you think they might want to discuss?

Mission and Dialogue

If someone is dismissed it means that he or she is sent away. The word mission also means sent, but sent to do a particular task. For Christians that mission is to preach the Gospel. They do it because Jesus told them to. His last words to the disciples, at the end of Matthew's Gospel, were:

> 'Go forth therefore and make all nations my disciples; baptize men everywhere in the name of the Father and the Son and the Holy Spirit, and teach them to observe all that I have commanded you. And be assured, I am with you always, to the end of time.'
>
> Matthew 28:19–20

Some time earlier in his ministry, Jesus had sent the disciples out in twos, about 70 of them, as a preparation for the work which was to begin after they had received the Holy Spirit (see Luke 9 and 10). The word apostle which was used of his twelve closest companions, and of Paul, means one who is sent.

The work of some early missionaries is discussed in Chapter 3. Here we take up the story in more modern times and concentrate on missionary work today. During the sixteenth century as Europeans began to explore regions which they had never known existed, like America, they also began to send missionaries to them. These missionaries were well intentioned and their work is often remembered with great gratitude. They attempted to soften the harshness of the colonisers who ill-treated and sometimes enslaved the nations which they conquered. However, they often confused the Gospel with western culture. So they brought Christianity but expected the converts to use European languages in worship, sing hymns to English, German or Spanish tunes, and replace their tribal customs and traditions with European dress, handshaking, robed choirs, organs, pianos and Christmas trees. Very few people, if any, saw anything wrong in this or in making moral demands such as expecting Christians to end polygamy*. Sometimes the missionaries made little attempt to learn languages and preached through interpreters. Not many of them studied the religions of those they came to evangelise.

*Polygamy is the practice of having more than one husband or wife. Polygyny is where one man has more than one wife and polyandry is where a woman has more than one husband.

Only recently has it been realised that what was happening, by accident rather than intention, was the devaluing of the cultures which the white Christians were encountering. Polygyny was practised to protect women in conditions where war or hunting might leave a woman destitute if her husband was killed (left a widow, she could become one of the wives of another man and so be provided for). Eating meat, which some Indian Christians did to imitate the people who had converted them, thinking it to be part of being a Christian, could separate them from their vegetarian families. They might be willing to accept the new religion, but not such a change in life style. These new churches also carried with them names which meant something in Europe, like Lutheran, Methodist, Roman Catholic and Presbyterian, but they were meaningless in countries where the Reformation was never an issue. They also tended to be served by European leaders, as if the converts and their descendants could not be trusted to look after their own affairs.

In the twentieth century missionary attitudes tend to be very different. Knowledge of languages and an understanding of the beliefs and cultures that will be met in the region to which the missionary is going are essential. The traditions of the potential convert are valued. It is the Christian faith which the missionary seeks to share, not western values and ways. An important verse of the Bible which they have in mind is, 'And you, like the lamp, must shed light among your fellows, so that, when they see the good you do, they may give praise to your Father in heaven' (Matthew 5:16).

Most missionaries do not now believe that they are bringing light to people who were living in spiritual darkness. They acknowledge that God was already there before they came. They also realise that it is their task to build up the local church as quickly as possible and then leave. Great missionaries of the past gave their lives to Africa, India, China, or whichever country they went to, often dying there after 30 or 40 years during which they may have only returned to Europe once or twice for a few months. Now they try to work themselves out of a job!

A missionary at work in the Omdurman Desert, Sudan.

Bishops attending the Lambeth Conference of the Anglican Church in 1988.

At the Lambeth Conference of the Anglican Church in 1988, there were more black bishops than white. In the Roman Catholic Church there are many cardinals who are not of European ancestry. In the churches they represent it is possible to find Christians being called to worship by drums not bells, rubbing noses (that is, sharing breath) rather than shaking hands as a sign of peace in a communion service, and singing hymns composed in the local language, set to regional tunes and played on traditional instruments.

1   Read and make notes about some of the great missionaries of the past, such as Hudson Taylor, St Francis Xavier, William Carey or Albert Schweitzer.
2   Why do you think Christians become missionaries? Obtain some modern missionary society pamphlets and compare the approaches with those of the past.
3   Invite a missionary to school to discuss his or her work with you.

DIALOGUE

Dialogue is a fairly new word but it refers to something which Christians have been doing since Jesus was a man, or even a boy. The only information the New Testament provides about Jesus' youth is the story of him listening and putting questions to the teachers in the Temple at Jerusalem (Luke 2:46). That is one kind of religious dialogue – listening and questioning.

Inter-religious dialogue requires:
● Meeting – Dialogue can take place when a person of one faith reads a book about another faith, written by one of its members. However, it is much more interesting when people actually get together and talk about their faiths, perhaps visit one another's place of worship or home.

- Trust and understanding – I must be honest with the person I am talking to and not secretly want to convert him or her.
- Respect – I must respect the other person as a human being as well as their beliefs and values.

Dialogue cannot happen when believers keep quiet about their faith. It would be opting out of dialogue if Christians said nothing about the things which matter to them and the Muslims or Sikhs they were talking to remained politely silent about their cherished beliefs.

There can be many reasons for dialogue. It may be to understand one another better. It may be to broaden one's spirituality by discovering what prayer or practising yoga means to someone of another faith. It may be to make the locality a safer and happier place for the people who live in it. Those who have taken part in dialogue, however, will agree that it changes their outlook, that the destination cannot be predicted in advance, and that the journey is probably more exciting than the place they thought they were heading for anyway.

Discuss:
a) Why are honesty, openness and respect essential in dialogue?
b) Why, in dialogue, is it more important to be a listener than a talker?
c) Are mission and dialogue alternatives?

Christian Teachings: Beliefs

Christian teaching is concerned with two matters:
- what Christians should *believe*
- how Christians should *live* (ethics).

THE TEACHING OF THE APOSTLES

The big argument that the early Christians had to consider was whether Jesus was the Messiah or not. Christ is the Greek form of this word, and the followers of Jesus were nicknamed Christians by Greek-speaking Jews because of the claim that Jesus was the Messiah, the Lord's anointed.

However, the apostles were not content to deal only with that issue, they saw it as important to claim that the Messiah would be sent by God to deliver people from the guilt of their sins. He would not be the Messiah of Jewish expectations who would defeat the Romans and establish a new kingdom like that of King David, based on Jerusalem. The keystone of their argument was that Jesus had been unjustly put to death, and that God had raised him back to life to demonstrate the truth of his claims to be God's deliverer. The men and women they persuaded would need to know how to live out their faith, but the first task of the apostles was to convince people that Jesus was God's chosen one, not a criminal who deserved to be executed. Only when they had successfully dealt with these matters would questions of ethics become important.

The apostle Peter concentrated on these issues when he made a public speech in Jerusalem to a crowd of people many of whom had probably witnessed the death of Jesus (Acts 2:22–36).

Peter and the other Christians claimed that Jesus was more than the Messiah, he was Lord. Lord was a term used to denote divinity. In the Roman world it was a title of the God emperor; among Jews *Adonai*, Lord, was a word used in addressing God.

1 Write *two* brief letters to a friend. In the first one imagine you are a Christian who was converted by Peter's speech; in the second imagine you were not converted.
2 Now imagine that you are the person who received both letters. Reply to them both.

Paul, the other great apostle, wrote letters to many of the Christian communities which he had established. One, in Corinth, seems to have forgotten what he taught it about Jesus. He wrote these words as a reminder:

> First and foremost, I handed on to you the facts which had been imparted to me: that Christ died for our sins, in accordance with the scriptures; that he was buried; that he was raised to life on the third day, according to the scriptures; and that he appeared to Cephas [the Aramaic form of Peter], and afterwards to the Twelve. Then he appeared to over five hundred of our brothers at once, most of whom are still alive . . .
>
> I Corinthians 15:3–6

The proof of the Resurrection clearly lay in questioning witnesses and in the experience of receiving the Holy Spirit which Paul refers to elsewhere in this letter. Only through this spiritual conviction was it possible to say 'Jesus is Lord' (I Corinthians 12:3). Both Peter and Paul used this brief statement, 'Jesus is Lord.' It seems to have been the first creed of the Christians. A creed is a statement of belief (from the Latin *credo* meaning 'I believe'). These three words sum up the points made by the two apostles in their teaching and speeches.

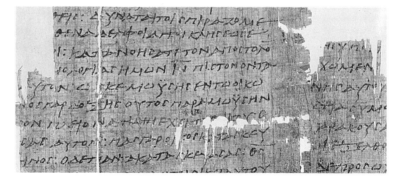

Part of the Letter to the Hebrews written on papyrus reeds. (What is the connection with paper?) If you look carefully you may make out the shape of the reeds.

The Apostles' Creed

With the passage of time Christians felt a need to spell out their beliefs in greater detail. One of their scholars Irenaeus, a Celtic-speaking bishop in Gaul (France), writing round about the year 190 CE, mentioned a rule of faith which all Christians accepted:

> The Church, though dispersed throughout the whole world, even to the ends of the earth, has received from the apostles and their disciples this faith: belief in one God, the father almighty, who made the heavens and earth and the seas and all that are in them; and in one Jesus Christ, the Son of God, who became incarnate for our salvation; and in the Holy Spirit, who proclaimed through the prophets the birth from a virgin, the passion and the resurrection from the dead, and the bodily ascension into heaven of our beloved Christ Jesus our Lord, and his future manifestation from heaven to sum up all things and raise up anew all flesh of the whole human race.

There was a need for this kind of statement because people were involved in debates about such things as whether Jesus was a real human being or just a spirit which appeared to be human, whether he really died, and whether Christians needed to keep their bodies pure. If they simply rotted in the ground after death then surely there was no harm in abusing them with drugs, alcohol or sexual immorality? The body did not matter. Irenaeus is saying that all Christians believe the body *is* important – that in Jesus God took human form and that the day will come when the dead will rise with renewed bodies, perhaps not the bodies they had possessed, but related, as the plant is to the seed.

The debates went on, especially during the years after 313 CE when Christianity became a legally recognised religion in the Roman Empire. Many people now joined not so much because they had a personal faith but because it was the right thing to do. It was fashionable, the old religions were not. Were there three gods or one? This was the kind of question the philosophers might challenge theologians with. New converts might ask something much nearer the heart: what about relatives who had died either before the time of Jesus or without hearing about him and therefore with no chance to become Christians?

The result was that bishops and other theologians held meetings called *councils* in order to decide what the true teachings or doctrines of the church were. Such assemblies had not been possible before in the days when Christianity was not recognised as a legal religion and its members were often in danger of persecution. Now things were so changed that those attending the councils were given imperial financial support and were able to use the imperial communications system which operated from one end of the empire to the other. One of the most important of the councils took place at Nicaea in what is now Turkey, not far from the new imperial capital of Constantinople. It eventually produced a rather detailed and complicated creed known as the Nicene Creed:

> We believe in one God, the Father Almighty, maker of heaven and earth, of all that is seen and unseen.
>
> We believe in one Lord, Jesus Christ, the only Son of God, eternally begotten of the Father, God from God, Light from Light, true God from true God, begotten not made, of one Being with the Father. Through him all things were made.
>
> For us men and for our salvation came down from heaven; by the power of the Holy Spirit he became incarnate of the Virgin Mary, and was made man. For our sake he was crucified under Pontius Pilate; he suffered and was buried.
>
> On the third day he rose again in accordance with the scriptures; he ascended into heaven, and is seated on the right hand of the Father. He will come in glory to judge the living and the dead, and his kingdom will have no end.

We believe in the Holy Spirit, the Lord, the giver of life, who proceeds from the Father *and the Son*. With the Father and the Son he is worshipped and glorified.

He has spoken through the Prophets.

We believe in one holy catholic and apostolic Church.

We acknowledge one baptism for the forgiveness of sins.

We look for the resurrection of the dead, and the life of the world to come. Amen.

Alternative Service Book, 1980

(The words in italics were added by the western catholic Church and influenced the split which took place in 1054, see page 27. Some versions use 'I' instead of 'we'.)

A more popular creed to appear during this period was one which became known as the Apostles' Creed because it was thought to sum up the teachings of Apostles as found in the New Testament. It was first referred to by this name by St Ambrose, bishop of Milan, in a letter written about 390 CE. He may have believed the legend that it was produced by the Apostles themselves. It reads:

I believe in God, the Father almighty, creator of heaven and earth. I believe in Jesus Christ, his only son, our Lord. He was conceived by the power of the Holy Spirit and born of the Virgin Mary. He suffered under Pontius Pilate, he was crucified, died, and was buried. He descended to the dead. On the third day he rose again. He ascended into heaven, and is seated at the right hand of the Father. He will come again to judge the living and the dead.

I believe in the Holy Spirit, the holy catholic Church, the communion of saints, the forgiveness of sins, the resurrection of the body, and life everlasting. Amen.

Alternative Service Book

(Sometimes 'we' is used instead of 'I' believe).

CHRISTIAN BELIEFS

God

The creed is about God first of all. He is the creator of the universe. Everything that exists has come about as a result of his decision and activity. He is also called father. This means that God is not a distant being who takes no interest in humanity. He is not one who started everything off and then left it to look after itself. God is like a good father, caring and interested in every human being. They are his children.

These beliefs about God do not necessarily mean that God is really male as opposed to female. God is personal according to Christian teaching. That means God cares, listens, helps people and is interested in their welfare. In the ancient world there were cults of female gods but these were often linked with fertility rituals which Jewish prophets denounced as immoral. Judaism therefore called God 'he'; Jesus as a Jew followed the tradition, and like other Jews called God *abba* meaning father, so Christians use these words when they speak of God or speak to God.

Jesus

Secondly the creed is about Jesus. He too is God. Christians talk about him being the Son of God. This is their way of trying to explain the relationship between Jesus and God the Father. The things Jesus did – caring for the sick, befriending the lonely and poor – were his genuine concerns, but they were also the kinds of thing that mattered to God, because God was in Jesus. Jesus was also human. He was born like other human beings, he suffered as they do, and he really died. The creed also says he descended to the dead and ascended to heaven. It was common belief at this time that below the earth was a place to which the dead went. Perhaps the idea was linked to the practice of western cultures of placing the dead in the ground, burying them. The suggestion that Jesus, after his death visited the abode of the dead is found in the first letter of St Peter (I Peter 3:18–19), where it says he preached to the imprisoned spirits. This was a way of explaining how people who had died before the time of Jesus could have a chance of salvation. Above the earth was heaven, so Jesus, raised from the dead and his mission accomplished, returned to his father by ascending into heaven. There he will remain until the Day of Judgement.

The Day of Judgement

Many Christians, but not all, believe that this world will eventually come to an end. Then those who are already dead, and those still living, will be divided into those who live eternally with God and those who are banished from his presence. Some Christians believe this happens at the death of an individual. Others think it is an ongoing process which occurs throughout a person's lifetime (see Matthew 25 and Revelation 20:11–15).

The Holy Spirit

However, Christians do not believe that Jesus deserted them and left them alone. They believe in the presence and power of the Holy Spirit. In other words, the energy and wisdom which the disciples of Jesus saw in him and which are described in the New Testament are still to be found in the Church and in the lives of men and women. Thirdly, then, the creed is about the Holy Spirit.

'God the Father, God the Son, and God the Holy Spirit' – Christians say there is one God, however, not three. This may be a difficult idea to grasp. Perhaps we can think of someone we know, possibly a friend. She or he is the daughter or son of his or her parents, also, your friend – and a student. Yet this person is not three but one. So with the Trinity, which is the name Christians give to God the Father, God the Son, and God the Holy Spirit. Experience taught the Apostles and believers ever since that there is one God, not three.

Who is the Holy Spirit?

The idea of the Holy Spirit probably has its origins in the experiences of the early Christians for which they could provide no explanation: incidents such as Jesus appearing to Paul on the road to Damascus (Acts 9); the rushing wind and tongues of fire experienced by the disciples at Pentecost (Acts 2); Peter's dream at Joppa (Acts 10); the healing powers which Christians found they sometimes possessed (Acts 3:1–10). These are ways in which they believed that God made himself known to them. It is a concept which some people have found it difficult to come to terms with. Examples of such experiences are still to be found today, especially where Christianity is new such as in parts of Africa.

In less dramatic, but no less real, ways Christians experienced the presence and power of the Holy Spirit. They were very much aware of this when a person was baptised. At first this often took a very dramatic form and the convert was almost visibly 'filled with the power of the Holy Spirit' (Acts 10:44–6). Later, this became less commonplace, as it is today, but not unknown. They were also conscious of this presence and power when they worshipped, especially when they broke bread, re-enacting the Last Supper.

The Communion of Saints

The creed also refers to 'the communion of saints'. These are not figures in stained glass windows, special people who are somehow different from most Christians. Saints in the New Testament sense are all those who seek to follow Jesus. The communion of saints is the fellowship of Christians living now on earth and eternally in the presence of God.

1 Memorise the Apostles' Creed.
2 What are the most important things that the creed says about:
 a) God?
 b) Jesus?
 c) the Holy Spirit?
3 What is the 'communion of saints'?

The Forgiveness of Sins

The phrase 'the forgiveness of sins' serves as a reminder that forgiveness was an important message which Jesus taught by word and by deed, and that one of the reasons for his death and resurrection was to assure people that God is forgiving.

The Resurrection of the Body

Surprisingly the Apostles' Creed does not say much about the meaning of Jesus' death, but the Nicene Creed says Jesus came down from heaven 'for us men and our salvation'. Christians believe that this was the whole purpose of the Incarnation, that is of God becoming human. Irenaeus (see page 86) said, 'He [Jesus] became what we are so that we might become what he is.' He showed human beings how to become perfect like himself, and gave them the ability to become perfect through receiving the Holy Spirit, especially in the sacraments, most notably the Eucharist (see page 36).

In fact, Irenaeus said that Jesus went through a whole process of putting things right. Adam, in the Bible story (Genesis 2–4), had disobeyed God by eating the fruit which he was forbidden to eat. Jesus had obeyed God; he had always done his will. Before eating the fruit Adam had given in to temptation. Jesus successfully resisted temptation in the wilderness. Adam had finally died and that was the end of his life. Jesus had died only to rise from the grave. In brief, Jesus had restored to humanity the opportunity to be as God wished it to be.

Of course all the consequences of what people do cannot ever be removed completely. We cannot call our words or our actions back once they have left us. Death having come into the world it had to remain, but Christians believe that Jesus stopped it being the end of the story and by his own resurrection, gave hope to humanity. This kind of interpretation of the purpose of Jesus' death became popular among eastern Christians. Western Christians have developed the ideas mentioned earlier (pages 10–11) much more.

He Will Come Again

A sentence in the creed which has certainly caused as much discussion as any other and probably more than most is 'He shall come again to judge the living and the dead.' The problem begins in the New Testament itself. Jesus preached the coming of the Kingdom of God. His followers expected it to be the climax of his ministry. Instead they saw Jesus die on a cross. The resurrection renewed their hopes, so we read in the Ascension story of them asking Jesus, 'Lord, is this the time when you are to establish once again the sovereignty of Israel?' He answered, 'It is not for you to know about dates or times, which the Father has set within his own control' (Acts 1:6–7).

Nevertheless, the Apostles encouraged Christians to be prepared for the return of Jesus when the kingdom would be established with power, especially when they were in danger of losing hope because of persecution. For example, in the first letter of Peter, there are the words:

Praise be to the God and Father of our Lord Jesus Christ, who in his mercy gave us new birth into a living hope by the resurrection of Jesus Christ from the dead! The inheritance to which we are born is one thing nothing can destroy or spoil or wither. It is kept for you in heaven, and you, because you put your faith in God, are under the protection of his power until salvation comes – the salvation which is even now in readiness and will be revealed at the end of time.

I Peter 1:3-5

Jehovah's Witnesses

Many Christians tend to think of the return of Jesus, the last time or the second coming as it is often called, as an inner experience, a condition in the hearts of Christians, but there are many others who expect it to be an actual historical event. One of the most famous groups of Christians to hold this belief are the Jehovah's Witnesses. Charles Taze Russell (1852–1916) was the founder of this movement of Bible Christians. They began in the United States but are now to be found world-wide. They are inspired to evangelise because of the command of Jesus to preach the gospel (the promise of the coming of God's Kingdom) to the whole world, but their sense of urgency comes from a belief that humanity is living in the age of ungodliness portrayed in the Revelation of John in the New Testament. The war between Satan and God (Jehovah) is imminent. A great battle of Armageddon, prophesied in Revelation 16:14–16, will take place, and afterwards there will be a new heaven and a new earth (Revelation 21:1), where the upright and perfect will live in peace, obeying God's will. In one of their hymns they express it in these words:

> A paradise our God has promised
> By means of Christ's millenial reign,
> When he'll blot out all sin and error,
> Removing death and tears and pain.
> A paradise the earth will be.
> With eyes of faith this can we see.
> This promise Christ shall soon fulfil,
> For he delights to do God's will.
>
> From the Jehovah's Witness hymn book,
> *Sing Praises to Jehovah*

The hymns of the Jehovah's Witnesses are based upon biblical passages. This one was inspired by Luke 23:43.

Write a sentence in answer to each of the following questions:
a)   What is the meaning of the word Messiah?
b)   What is the Greek word meaning Messiah?
c)   Why did Christians prefer the word Lord?
d)   What did Christians mean when they said, 'Jesus is Lord'?
e)   What is a creed?
f)   What important event for Christians took place in 313 CE?
g)   Name the first Christian emperor.
h)   Who is Jehovah?
i)   What is 'Christ's millenial reign' mentioned in the hymn sung by Jehovah's Witnesses?

<table>
<tr><td>

Chapter

13

</td><td>

Christian Teaching: Ethics

</td></tr>
</table>

When someone asked Jesus to tell him the essence of his Jewish faith, Jesus asked him what he thought. He answered, 'Love the Lord your God with all your heart, with all your soul, with all your strength, and with all your mind; and your neighbour as yourself.' 'That is the right answer,' said Jesus; 'do that and you will live' (Luke 10:27–8).

Since then the two great principles of Christianity have been to love God and to love your neighbour. The first, loving God, covers things like worship and vocation, that is deciding what kind of work one should do. The second has to do with behaviour and conduct, especially relationships with other people, and covers such subjects as poverty, the family, prejudice, racism, and peace and war.

We have already learned that the first Christians were Jews. Their religion provided such a fine code of conduct that some Gentiles converted to it or at least worshipped in the synagogues and modelled their private lives upon Jewish teachings. The ethics of Judaism are contained in the five books of Moses in the Old Testament (Genesis, Exodus, Leviticus, Numbers and Deuteronomy), where there are no less than 613 commandments, and the prophetic books, such as Jeremiah or Amos. Not all the 613 commandments are on the subject of social conduct, but many are. The most famous are six of the ten commandments:

> Honour your father and your mother . . .
> You shall not commit murder.
> You shall not commit adultery.
> You shall not steal.
> You shall not give false witness against your neighbour.
> You shall not covet your neighbour's house . . . wife, his slave, his slave-girl, his ox, his ass, or anything that belongs to him.
>
> Exodus 20:12–17

Laws can be so harsh that they can actually result in injustice or cruelty. There is the famous punishment in Exodus, 'an eye for an eye and a tooth for a tooth' (Exodus 21:22–5), but the religious teachers of Judaism pointed out that anyone who did that, even legally, was disfiguring a human being who was created in the image of God. It is said, 'You shall observe my institutions and my laws; the man who keeps them shall have life through them' (Leviticus 18:5). This means that the purpose of the commandments was not to crush the human spirit, but to liberate it.

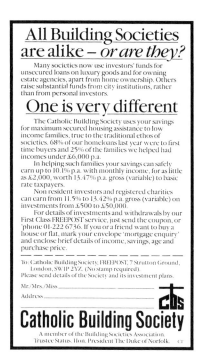

A Christian ethical investment advertisement.

The prophets shared this view. The instructions contained in the books of Moses were not to be set aside, but obeyed in spirit, not just letter. One of them, Micah, said, 'It has been told you what is good, and what is it that the Lord asks of you? Only to act justly, to love mercy, and to walk humbly with your God' (Micah 6:8). These were the kinds of teachings that the disciples of Jesus had been brought up to follow. He reinforced the message of the prophets in his own teaching, especially in what is known as the Sermon on the Mount (Matthew 5, 6 and 7). He emphasised the spirit of the law by saying such things as, 'You have learned that our forefathers were told, "Do not commit murder; anyone who commits murder must be brought to judgement." But what I tell you is this: Anyone who nurses anger against his brother must be brought to judgement' (Matthew 5:21–2). The ethical teaching of Jesus stressed love, mercy and forgiveness. He even said, 'If someone slaps you on the right cheek, turn and offer him your left' (Matthew 5:39).

The New Testament is concerned with personal ethics, especially the way one Christian should treat another. There was no point in commenting upon the great issues of the day, such as the use of torture, throwing criminals to the wild beasts in Roman amphitheatres, or the gladiatorial games which took place there, or even the injustice and inhumanity of slavery. Christians did not have power to change social conditions. Paul did write to Philemon, a slave-owner, asking him to treat a runaway Christian slave mercifully, but he did not even suggest that he should set him free. It was only in 1833 that slavery was abolished in the territories which Britain then ruled, and in 1865 in the USA.

Christians today still struggle to discover what is right in matters of personal conduct. Are there jobs which they should not do? Some would not work for a football pools firm or a betting shop, because they believe that gambling is wrong. Others might not join one of the armed forces, or work in a public house. Those who can save money may debate whether to invest it in stocks and shares or building societies, where it may be of more help to people trying to buy their own homes. A few may rid themselves of the problem by giving away their surplus income altogether.

?

List some of the sayings and actions of Jesus which Christians might have in mind when faced with moral dilemmas.
a) How might they be helped by them?
b) Why might a Christian find some jobs unacceptable?
c) Which kinds of jobs might a Christian find most acceptable?

Chapter 14

Vocation

For some time the first Christians lived each day as if it were their last and believed that the Jesus who had left them at the Ascension would return very soon in triumph. St Paul preached this message so strongly that some Christians may have given up work altogether to prepare for it. He had to write to the church in Thessalonica, 'the man who will not work shall not eat' (2 Thessalonians 3:10).

It has always been a Christian principle that people should work for a living and not depend on the kindness of others. The story in the Book of Genesis about the expulsion of Adam and Eve from the Garden of Eden tells of them being condemned to earn a living. God says, 'Cursed is the ground because of you; in toil you shall eat of it all the days of your life . . . In the sweat of your face shall you eat bread till you return to the ground' (Genesis 3:17–19). Whether Christians understand the story literally or not, they recognise that work is necessary and proper.

Christians sometimes talk about their vocation. The word simply means calling and refers to the belief that God has work for them to do and calls them to do it. He speaks to them through such things as prayer, the Bible, friends, perhaps a film they have seen or a magazine article they have read, and they respond. Vocation is sometimes used only in a special sense, to refer to a calling to become a priest or a nun, perhaps a teacher or nurse, but the real Christian belief is that God has a vocation for *everyone*. To be a reliable postman, bus driver or refuse collector, requires as much faith as to be a priest, especially if the job is one which society does not value, even though it is essential. Christians should not regard one vocation or occupation as superior to another.

Not all work can be classed as suitable for a Christian to do. Obviously, it would be regarded as wrong to live off immoral earnings, or theft. Some would include gambling, running a pub, or even being a regular in the armed forces, as unacceptable. Usually Christians speak of at least three criteria in considering the question of vocation:

- Is the job necessary?
- Is it honest?
- Does it benefit other people?

Work which is harmful to others or is self-indulgent is often thought to be wrong. Also we should not require others to do jobs which are degrading. Feminist Christians for example agree with other women that they should not be exploited sexually to sell cars, yachts, or newspapers.

In recent years there seems to have been less emphasis upon right and wrong kinds of work because some things are now considered less harmful than in the past. It is realised that people need not drink to excess, 'the demon drink' which William Booth and others condemned need not destroy lives; social drinking is possible. There is also an awareness that work is often a complex matter. For example, if a person thought that the tobacco trade was wrong, he might refuse to take a job in a factory making cigarettes. Should he also refuse to attend a cricket match sponsored by a tobacco company, or take part in an athletics meeting which they had supported? His bank might have investments in the firm, should he change banks – perhaps only to find that his new choice has shares in a brewery or an armament firm? However, the Christian is not supposed to 'cop out' of making a decision just because it is difficult.

Remember, Christianity leaves much to the individual conscience. What one person regards as acceptable another may consider to be wrong.

?

1   List some jobs which Christians might consider unacceptable forms of employment. What reasons might they give?
2   List some jobs which Christians might regard as highly acceptable. Again give the reasons they might give.
3   Think of some jobs which are debatable. Research them as carefully as you can, then hold a class discussion and list the arguments which you consider the best on both sides.
4   If possible invite some Christians to school to tell you why they chose their particular occupations. Notice how it is possible for Christians to share the same faith but come to different conclusions on ethical matters. This is especially true of attitudes to serving in the armed forces.

Since the time of the Emperor Constantine, Christians have often been in positions of influence and power, and have been able to give attention to social issues. In Chapters 15–19 we will look at personal and social ethics which are important today.

Chapter 15

Poverty and Wealth

Francis of Assisi (1181–1226) spoke of 'embracing sister Poverty'. He visited Rome on pilgrimage, exchanged clothes with a beggar, spent a day begging, and decided to live as simply as possible for the rest of his life and to help the poor. His father, a rich merchant, disowned him.

Not many Christians have gone to the extremes of St Francis, but the issues of poverty and wealth exercise the minds and consciences of most Christians. Christianity, like its parent Judaism, and other faiths, is a religion of caring. 'Love your neighbour as yourself' is a key teaching.

?

Collect information about St Francis and write a brief biography of him.

Jesus often warned people of the dangers of wealth. Here are some of his comments:

> Do not store up for yourselves treasure on earth, where it grows rusty and moth-eaten, and thieves break in to steal it. Store up treasure in heaven where there is no moth and no rust to spoil it, no thieves to break in and steal. For where your wealth is, there will your heart be also.
>
> Matthew 6:19–20

> No servant can be slave to two masters; for either he will hate the first and love the second, or he will be devoted to the first and think nothing of the second. You cannot serve God and Money.
>
> Matthew 6:24

This is the answer Jesus gave to a rich young man who asked him how he might achieve eternal life, 'Go, sell everything you have, and give to the poor, and you will have riches in heaven; and come, follow me' (Mark 10:21). And these words were spoken to someone whose brother was not sharing his inheritance with him, 'Be on your guard against greed of every kind, for even when a man has more than enough, his wealth does not give him life' (Luke 12:15).

But perhaps the most famous words on the subject were spoken by St Paul, 'The love of money is the root of all evil things' (1 Timothy 6:10). It is not wealth in itself that is wrong, but greed, for that means

Mother Theresa is famous for her work among the homeless in Calcutta. Here she is seen going to meet the homeless in London.

that the desire to have possessions takes priority over eagerness to serve God. That is why the young man in the verse from Mark's Gospel was advised to give everything away.

The divide between rich and poor has absorbed much of the attention and the efforts of Christians in the second half of the twentieth century. In 1945, at the end of the Second World War, the allies realised that people in Germany, Holland, and some other countries on mainland Europe, would starve to death unless they were given help urgently. Supplies, and volunteers to distribute them, were sent. It soon became clear that similar needs existed in other parts of the world. Out of this awareness Christian Aid was born. It is now one of several Christian organisations working to help people in need world-wide; others include CAFOD and Tear Fund. They are part of the recognition that poverty is a crime against humanity as long as there are rich individuals and rich nations who can prevent it.

?

Collect newspaper advertisements from Christian care agencies. Write to some of them for publicity material. Mount what you can obtain as part of a classroom exhibition on poverty and wealth. You might be able to paint some posters of your own.

Jesus often told his followers, or rich people who came to hear him, that they should care for the poor but one of the most important statements is contained in the letter of the Apostle James:

> My brothers, what use is it for a man to say he has faith when he does nothing to show it? Can that faith save him? Suppose a brother or sister is in rags with not enough food for the day, and one of you says, 'Good luck to you, keep yourselves warm and have plenty to eat, but does nothing to supply their bodily needs, what is the good of that? So with faith; if it does not lead to action, it is in itself a lifeless thing.

James 2:14–17

However, the aim of aid is not simply to prevent other people from starving, it is to help them to feed themselves, find employment and recover their dignity as human beings. Although Christian Aid and the other organisations are frequently described as 'relief agencies', and are only heard of in times of crisis when there are floods or earthquakes, much of their work goes unnoticed for 365 days each year and takes the form of self-help programmes.

There are many motives for providing aid. St Paul said that the one essential was love, 'I may dole out all I possess, or even give my body to be burnt, but if I have not love I am none the better' (I Corinthians 13:3). Martin Luther King, a great Christian civil rights leader made a similar point. He said, 'As long as there is poverty in the world I can never be rich, even if I have a million dollars. I can never be what I ought to be until you are what you ought to be.'

Discuss why, for the Christian, wealth and its uneven distribution is not just an economic issue.

Christians are not only involved in helping the needy in Asia, Africa, or South America, but also those in their own countries. For example, in Britain the Reverend Chad Varah, an Anglican priest, started an organisation called the Samaritans in 1953. They provide a confidential telephone service; volunteers counsel and befriend people who are suicidal and despairing. Group Captain Cheshire VC, a Roman Catholic, began caring for the terminally ill after the Second World War; the result has been the Cheshire Homes. His wife, Sue Ryder, has encouraged similar work.

1   Find out what examples of caring you can find being carried out by Christians in your country or the area where you live? Volunteers are busy people but you may be able to persuade someone to visit the school and speak to you.
2   Write down and learn all the New Testament passages about poverty and wealth mentioned in this chapter. Leave space to add any more you come across.
3   Produce an assembly on 'Christians, poverty and wealth' lasting 10 or 15 minutes. (You may be able to persuade friends doing Geography or other subjects to produce one from their standpoint in the same week.) If you are studying another religion as well as Christianity, its insights could also be given as part of a series of assemblies.
4   Try to arrange a visit to your school by a Franciscan, or some other nun or monk working among the poor in Britain.

Chapter
16

The Family

FAMILY

Jesus' idea of the family went beyond blood relationship. Once, when his mother and brothers came to see him, he said, 'Who is my mother? Who are my brothers?' And looking round at those who were sitting in the circle about him he said, 'Here are my mother and my brothers. Whoever does the will of God is my brother, my sister, my mother' (Mark 3:33–5).

Jesus also warned his followers that discipleship might mean having to choose between him and family. At one time Roman Catholic priests and nuns might never have seen their relatives again after taking holy orders. They were likely to be sent far from them. This happens less now than it did 50 years ago, but missionaries of all denominations may be parted from their parents for many years. They are likely to be accompanied by their husband or wife, but their children may go to boarding schools in the home country.

However, Jesus was probably thinking about something even more serious. Religious beliefs can end friendships and even break up families. Chapter 17 shows how strong Jewish and Christian hostility could become, and there were Jews who disagreed so much with Jesus that they plotted his death. St Paul might have been prepared to arrest Christian members of his own family (if there were any) before his conversion. After it some of them might have refused to have anything more to do with him. It is this kind of thing which Jesus had in mind when he spoke some very harsh words:

> 'If anyone comes to me and does not hate his father and mother, wife and children, brothers and sisters, even his own life, he cannot be a disciple of mine.'

Luke 14:26

? Look up Matthew 10:37–8. Why do you think he used 'cares more' instead of 'hate'? Which do you think is more likely to have been spoken by Jesus?

Most Christians for much of the time did not find life so demanding. Persecution was fairly rare and the Christian slave, master, trader or farmer, lived a normal life. St Paul felt the need to write about family matters in a number of his letters. In the first of his letters to Timothy, his friend and fellow missionary, he attacks some Christians who apparently told people not to marry but to remain celibate (1 Timothy 4:3). In the same letter he recommended that young widows should remarry otherwise they might become the focus of gossip and earn the church a bad name (1 Timothy 5:14). Older widows should be looked after by their children or other relatives. Widows over 60 with no one to care for them should be supported by the congregation (1 Timothy 5:3–10).

Clearly, he accepted the teaching of the fifth of the ten command-ments, 'Honour your father and your mother' (Exodus 20:12) and also the advice given in the book of Proverbs, 'Listen to your father who gave you life, and do not despise your mother when she is old' (Proverbs 23:22). In his letter to the Ephesian church he actually quoted the verse from Exodus, and wrote, 'Children, obey your parents' (Ephesians 6:1).

MARRIAGE

St Paul did not live at a time of sexual and social equality. He instructed wives to obey their husbands:

> Wives, be subject to your husbands as to the Lord; for man is the head of the woman, just as Christ also is head of the church. . . . but just as the church is subject to Christ, so must women be to their husbands in everything.
>
> Ephesians 5:22–4

However, he did continue to tell husbands that they must love their wives 'as they love their own bodies' (5:28).

The view of St Paul is a matter of debate among Christians today. Many Bible Christians accept what he wrote. The husband is head of the family and the wife respectfully obeys him. However, other Christians would say that Paul was writing as a man of his time. His words do not apply today. The Anglican marriage service in the *Book of Common Prayer* requires the bride to 'love, honour, and obey' her husband. 'Obey' is missing from the *Alternative Service Book* of 1980. The bride says she will 'Love, comfort, honour, and protect' her husband. This is exactly the same promise as he makes to her.

St Paul does not seem to have placed a very high importance upon marriage. He opposed sex outside it, but he thought that the single state was better, 'To the unmarried and to widows I say this: it is a good thing if they stay as I am myself; but if they cannot control themselves, they should marry' (1 Corinthians 7:8–9). (Compare his advice to widows here with that in his letter to Timothy.)

There is general agreement among the churches that there are three reasons for Christian marriage:
- To have children (sometimes marriage services mention the 'procreation' of children. This recognises that God is *the*

Creator, but has given human beings the privilege of sharing in the work of producing life.)
- To provide a right relationship for sexual intercourse
- To give one another help, comfort, and protection.

The Methodist Church in England sets out the purpose of marriage in these words:

> According to the teaching of Christ, marriage is the lifelong union in body, mind and spirit, of one man and one woman. It is his will that in marriage the love of man and woman should be fulfilled in the wholeness of their life together, in mutual companionship, helpfulness and care. By the help of God this love grows and deepens with the years. Such marriage is the foundation of true family life, and when blessed with the gift of children, is God's chosen way for the continuance of mankind and the bringing up of children in security and trust.
>
> Methodist Wedding Service Order

?

1   Discuss:
   a)   Does the Methodist statement include all the three reasons listed?
   b)   Which reason for marriage does it seem to consider most important?
2   Try to obtain some other statements and find out what reasons they give for Christian marriage.
3   If possible get a copy of the three reasons given at the beginning of the Solemnization of Marriage in the *Book of Common Prayer* and compare it with those mentioned in the Marriage Service in the *Alternative Service Book*. What differences can you discover? Can you suggest reasons for them?

The Christian ideal of marriage is that of one husband, one wife, for life. However, at the Lambeth Conference of Anglican bishops 1988 it was agreed that in certain circumstances polygamy (see page 80) might be permitted. In some areas of the world it is a normal feature of society. For example, in parts of Africa men have a number of wives (polygyny). The reasons for this vary. It may be social custom. It may be a way of giving women protection in cultures where men's lives are at risk because their ways of making a living are dangerous and lead to a high death rate. The women need to be provided for. Polygyny gives security. Sometimes Christian missionaries from Europe did not realise that this might be the purpose of polygyny and have required converts to get rid of all but one wife. This has brought shame upon the rejected wives and forced them to become beggars or prostitutes if their families would not care for them. The compromise on polygamy only applies to converts. Men or women who are already Christians when they marry must have only one partner.

Marriage customs vary from church to church and in different parts of the world. Find out about some of them and their Christian significance. For example, in India Christian brides may dress in red, whereas in European countries white is usual. Why? Sometimes couples exchange rings, or the groom gives one to the bride. Why? In some countries Christians have arranged marriages. What considerations are parents likely to take into account when looking for a partner for their son or daughter?

Alliance invited for Keralite Roman Catholic girl, aged 27, working in Austria as stenographer, from computer graduates, stenographers, bank employees, chartered accountants, etc. Write with details to Box No. XXX, *Times of India*, Bombay.

Syrian Christian parents, settled in USA, invite matrimonial correspond-ence for their son, aged 26, computer programmer doing Masters, from medical doctors, dentists, pharmacists or engineers, from Keralite Christians. Box No. XXX, *The Hindu*, Madras.

Indian families sometimes have to advertise to help them find marriage partners for their children.

An Indian Christian wedding. The couple sit together in front of the communion table.

DIVORCE

Not all Christian marriages are happy and successful. Christian teaching is often that the couple should stay together and work to rescue the marriage, helped by God's grace. Christians believe that no divorce is possible if the partners have promised to live together as man and wife 'till death us do part', as marriage services sometimes put it. Strictly speaking the Roman Catholic Church does not accept divorce but it does recognise certain reasons for annulment (that is saying that it was never a valid marriage) or for nullifying it. Grounds for nullity are refusal to consummate a marriage, insanity, venereal disease in a form which might be passed on to the spouse, and pregnancy by a person other than the husband.

Mark's Gospel asserts that Jesus rejected divorce completely, and condemned remarriage. Jesus says, 'Whoever divorces his wife and marries another commits adultery against her: so too, if she divorces her husband and marries another, she commits adultery' (Mark 10:10–12). However, in Matthew's Gospel Jesus says something slightly different, 'I tell you, if a man divorces his wife for any cause other than unchastity, and marries another, he commits adultery' (Matthew 19:9). St Paul took the view that if the non-Christian partner in a mixed marriage wanted a separation the Christian should not prevent it, but otherwise it should be binding (1 Corinthians 7:15).

In some countries a Christian denomination which opposes divorce may use its influence to keep it illegal as it was in western Europe until the Reformation. An example of such a country is the Irish Republic. On the other hand Christians may feel that they should not prevent people who do not share their beliefs from having the right to divorce, though they are concerned about a society in which divorce is made easy. Others may hold the view that marriage is too easy, that vows are taken too lightly and that it should be more 'difficult' to get married. It is too late, and wrong, to put obstacles in the way of divorce when a marriage is breaking up.

Discuss:
a) What arguments might a Christian put forward for allowing divorce?
b) What arguments might a Christian put forward for saying that divorce should not be permitted?
c) How might Christians reply to someone who says they should not use their influence to prevent people having the right to divorce?

Most denominations accept divorce reluctantly as a fact of life. Some will allow a divorced person to remarry in church, others will not. In the Anglican Church divorced people remarrying may have a church blessing after a civil ceremony. While Christians do not wish to inflict misery upon couples whose marriage is dead in a practical sense, they do not want to give the impression that promises can be lightly made and easily broken. What other reasons might Christians give for opposing or permitting a divorced person to remarry in church?

<table>
<tr>
<td>

Chapter

17

</td>
<td>

Anti-Semitism

</td>
</tr>
</table>

Anti-Semitism, the name given to anti-Jewish attitudes and conduct, began very early in the history of Christianity, grew during the Middle Ages and reached its climax in the twentieth century.

The Garden of the Righteous, Yad Vashem, Jerusalem, where those who helped Jews during the Holocaust are remembered.

Christianity began, as we have seen, as a Jewish movement which held the belief that Jesus was the promised Messiah, but that he was also the saviour of all humanity who, on the cross, had taken away the sins of the whole world. However, before long Christians left the religion of their birth behind. Most of them were people with no Jewish heritage. The Greek and Roman cultures to which they belonged disliked and despised the Jews because they were monotheists who would not worship the emperor (monotheists believe in only one God), and because they also kept to their own traditions, often not intermarrying. Some Christians shared this hostility towards the Jews. Of course, the Church had suffered persecution itself until Constantine became emperor (see page 20), partly because it had the same views as the Jews on monotheism and emperor worship. Feelings about the Jews however remained the same. In 305 CE a council of Christians in Elvira in Spain decreed that Christians should not marry Jews or eat with them.

Many Jews came to England with William the Conqueror and settled in large towns and cities. They kept their communities separate from the English and became successful in business. As a result they were treated with suspicion. Their wealth gave them the reputation for avarice.

The Crusades (eleventh to thirteenth centuries) were instrumental in changing attitudes towards Jews for the worse. The Crusades were religious wars fought by Christian Europeans against the Turks (Saracens), followers of Islam. The aim was to ensure the safety of pilgrims visiting Palestine, which had been conquered by the Turks. Religious zeal was at its height whenever recruitment for the Crusades was happening. Those who did not go on the Crusades turned against the Jews who, they felt, were just as bad as the Saracens.

In 1189 a deputation of Jews appeared at Richard I's coronation and was attacked by the mob. A rumour spread that the King had ordered a massacre of Jews. These massacres occurred in the main cities and towns where Jews lived, such as London, Norwich, Stamford, King's Lynn and Lincoln. Some of the worst massacres occurred in York. In 1190 the Jews of York who had taken shelter in Clifford's Tower were burned to death. They may have chosen the way of mass suicide in preference to being killed by the mob which was besieging the tower.

The Fourth Lateran Council of the Roman Church, meeting in 1215, barred Jews from holding public office in Christian realms. It was thought wrong that 'a blasphemer of Christ should exercise authority over Christians'. Here we come to particularly Christian reasons for anti-Semitism – Jews would not accept that Jesus was the Messiah, they were considered to be responsible for the Crucifixion, and, it was thought, murdered children to use their blood in rituals. Hugh of Lincoln (*c.* 1246–55), Blessed Andrew of Rinn (1462) and Blessed Simon of Trent (1475) were three such boys whose disappearance was blamed on the local Jewish community without any justification. To hear that a Christian child had gone missing was bad news to Jews in the neighbourhood. (In 1965 the veneration of Simon of Trent was stopped. It was recognised that he had not been killed by Jews, and that his cult was a means of inflaming anti-Semitic feelings.)

England eventually expelled its Jewish citizens in 1290 and then when the government of Oliver Cromwell readmitted them in 1656 it was in the face of much opposition.

Find out where the Jewish community nearest to you is. When did it settle? Why? Where did the Jews come from? Try to discover whether there was a Jewish community before 1290 and collect any stories about it.

From the thirteenth century to the twentieth century Jews continued to be persecuted in various parts of the world. In Germany, for example, Martin Luther (see page 29) shared the common attitude towards Jews. In 1543 he wrote a pamphlet *Against the Jews and their Lies* in which he proposed that their synagogues should be burned, they should only be allowed to undertake manual work or, better still, princes should expel them from their countries. In his very last sermon he denounced the Jews for obstinately refusing to accept Jesus as their messiah and saviour, and called for their expulsion from Germany as a matter of urgency. In Russia between 1881 and 1910 at least 3 000 000 Jews fled from persecution, with a large majority of them ending up in the USA. They continued to be persecuted in Russia during the First World War.

The best-known aspect of anti-Semitism occurred in the twentieth century in Germany. Jews, together with Jesuits, freemasons, communists, Jehovah's Witnesses and gypsies, became the target of Hitler's campaign to establish an Aryan race. Propaganda was used to blame these groups for Germany's ills, the defeat of 1918 and the depression of the post-war period. Some Christians were deceived by what the state-controlled press and radio told them, but as early as 1933 the world's press was carrying accounts of violent attacks on Jews in Germany. Children were taught in German schools to regard these groups as evil and deserving of punishment. Other Christians who knew what was happening were traditionally anti-Semitic. By 1935 all Jews in Germany were deprived of their rights and sent to concentration camps, and thence to the gas chambers. Some, however, did manage to escape. Those who spoke out on behalf of the Jews shared their fate, at least to the extent of being thrown into the concentration camps, even if they escaped the gas chambers. In 1938 Pope Pius said, 'Anti-Semitism is a movement in which Christians can have no part whatsoever. Spiritually we are all Semites.' These words came too late to deter Hitler.

Awareness of what was happening in Nazi-occupied Europe reached other countries through refugees. In 1942 the Council of Christians and Jews was formed with the aim of promoting Jewish-Christian understanding so that the misunderstandings, distortions, and persecutions which had characterised relationships between the two faiths for so long could be eliminated.

?

1 What is a Semite?
2 What do you think Pope Pius XI meant by saying 'We are all Semites'?
3 If there is a Council of Christians and Jews near where you live, find out the kinds of thing they do.

When the leaders of the Roman Catholic Church met for the Second Vatican Council (1962–5) the relationship with Judaism was an important item on the agenda. The Council could not deny its faith in Jesus as Messiah and saviour but it did find a way of acknowledging the worth of Judaism and calling upon Christians to adopt a new attitude towards it. In a document entitled *Nostra Aetate* it said:

> As this Sacred Synod searches into the mystery of the Church, it remembers the bond that spiritually ties the people of the new covenant to Abraham's stock. Thus, the Church of Christ acknowledges that, according to God's saving design, the beginnings of her faith and election are found already among the patriarchs, Moses and the prophets. She believes that all those who believe in Christ – Abraham's sons according to faith – are included in the same patriarch's call, and likewise that the salvation of the church is mysteriously foreshadowed by the chosen people's exodus from the house of bondage. The church, therefore, cannot forget that she received the revelation of the Old Testament through the people with whom God in his inexpressible mercy concluded the ancient covenant. Nor can she forget that she draws sustenance from the roots of that well-cultivated olive tree unto which has been grafted the wild shoot, the Gentiles. Indeed the church believes that by his cross Christ, our peace, reconciled Jews and Gentiles, making both one in himself.

This is not an easy passage to read or understand, but its importance lies in its recognition that:

- Christians come from the 'stock' of Judaism
- Christians owe a debt to Judaism
- Jesus should be a reason for reconciliation not hostility.

?

Try to explain these three things in your own words.

Nostra Aetate also stated, 'In her rejection of every persecution against any man, the Church … decries hatred, persecutions, displays of antisemitism, directed against Jews at any time and by anyone.'

Christians are now united in opposing anti-Semitism, and a number of denominations have made statements similar to that of the Roman Catholic Church. However, there are still problems to be sorted out. When Pope Paul visited the USA in 1965 a Mass which he was celebrating included the passage from John 20:19, where it says the disciples of Jesus 'were gathered together for fear of the Jews'. Many viewers were upset as they watched the Mass on TV. The *Alternative Service Book* of the Church of England has a collect (prayer) for Good Friday which includes the words, 'Have mercy upon your ancient people the Jews, and upon all who have not known you, or deny the faith of Christ crucified; take from them all ignorance, hardness of heart, and contempt for your word.' This is better than the words of the Good Friday collect in the *Book of Common Prayer* which refers to 'Jews, Turks, Infidels, and Hereticks', but there is still room for improvement. The process of responding to Judaism at a practical level lags some way behind Christians theological statements.

?

Individually, or as a class, make a file on anti-Semitism. Divide it into four sections:

a)   Newspaper cuttings which are disrespectful to people of other countries and races. (One reason for anti-Semitism is dislike of 'foreigners', and Jews have suffered from this, having no country to call their own until recently.)

b)   A list of principles, beliefs and practices which make Jews distinctive from other social and religious groups. It may be possible to include photographs. (A second reason for anti-Semitism is that we do not like people who are different from us.)

c)   A list of reasons for Christian anti-Semitism, with passages from books if you can find any.

d)   A collection of material, especially Christian, which condemns anti-Semitism, and deals with the kinds of comments found in the other three sections.

Racism and Apartheid

Racism seems to be as old as history. To regard other families or races as inferior to our own seems to be a way in which we preserve loyalty and identity. If we are told that other people are wicked, dishonest and ready to harm us, we are more inclined to fight against them. If we think they are kind, good and have something positive to offer to our way of life, we might befriend them and even intermarry. Nationalism often thrives on suspicion of neighbouring countries. Language helps. Foreigner, alien, even barbarian, are the kinds of words found in dictionaries to describe the inhabitants of other countries.

Christianity does not itself approve of racism, but Christians have been manipulated in this respect from time to time, as they have in many other matters. Perhaps the key Christian statement was made by St Paul soon after he began preaching to non-Jews, 'There is no question here of Greek and Jew, circumcised and uncircumcised, barbarian, Scythian, freeman, slave; but Christ is all, and is in all' (Colossians 3:11). The issue was very important to Paul, so much so that he made a similar comment in another letter, this time to Corinth, 'For indeed we were all brought into one body by baptism, in the one Spirit, whether we are Jews or Greeks, whether slaves or free men, and that one Holy Spirit was poured out for all of us to drink' (1 Corinthians 12:13).

Slavery

Clearly Paul had a vision of one Gospel, one Saviour, one baptism in one Spirit, and consequently of one humanity. This did not prompt him to denounce slavery. It was an established institution and many Romans believed that the empire depended on it. However, slaves were men and women with souls who should be treated justly. He wrote to masters and slaves in the church at Colossus:

> Slaves, give entire obedience to your earthly masters, not merely with an outward show of service, to curry favour with men, but with single-mindedness, out of reverence for the Lord . . . Masters, be just and fair to your slaves, knowing that you too have a Master in heaven.
>
> Colossians 3:22–4:1

Roman slavery was not racial, though many of the slaves came from conquered tribes and nations. Many were of the same race as their owners. Gradually, during the Middle Ages, slavery was replaced by serfdom, which itself disappeared. However, the idea of slavery and the sense of inequality which went with it remained in the Bible which never challenged the notion that some people were born to rule and others to obey them.

Slavery remained in the Muslim world and large numbers of Christians who were captured at the fall of Constantinople in 1453 were enslaved. With the discovery or America, Portugese, Spanish and British settlers made slaves of the native Indians, and also began importing slaves from Africa, despite the opposition of missionaries and popes. Skin colour now became an element in the story. Some Christians denied that black people had souls.

?

Christianity has often been criticised as the 'white man's religion'. Write two letters in reply to this statement:
a)   one from a black person
b)   one from a white person.

APARTHEID

In the nineteenth century one group of Christians, the Dutch Reformed Church, searched the scriptures and found a biblical passage which permitted slavery and could even be used to argue that certain people should be enslaved. In Genesis 9 and 10 there is a strange story of one of the sons of Noah, called Ham, entering his father's tent and finding him asleep naked. In his culture this was highly improper. Ham's brothers, when he told them what he had seen, took a cloak, walked into the tent backwards and covered up Noah. When the father woke and discovered what had happened, he cursed Ham and his descendants, through Canaan (Ham's son):

An example of apartheid in South Africa.

Curse be Canaan,
slave of slaves
shall he be to
his brothers. . . .
Bless, O lord,
the tents of Shem;
may Canaan be
his slave.

Genesis 9:25–6

The story goes on to describe the migration of the families of the four sons of Noah to repopulate the earth after the Flood.

The Dutch Reformed Church of South Africa claimed that the children of Ham were the black tribes which they encountered in southern Africa. The white settlers were descendants of Shem, who had therefore a right to enslave them. When South Africa passed to the British and slavery was abolished, the Dutch, known as Boers, adopted a new policy of separate development based on the superiority of white over black. The system is called *apartheid* in Afrikaans, the language of the Boers.

An official pamphlet of the Nationalist Party (the political party of the Boers) which put forward the policy of apartheid and put it into effect when it came to power soon after the Second World War reads:

> The policy of apartheid should encourage total apartheid as the ultimate goal of a natural process of separate development. . . . It is the primary task and calling of the state to seek the welfare of South Africa, and to promote the happiness and well-being of its citizens, non-white as well as white. Realising that such a task can be best accomplished by preserving and safeguarding the white race, the Nationalist Party professes this as the guiding principle of its policy.

What this policy means is that power is in the hands of the white population of four million. The 19 million blacks have no vote. Whites own 87 per cent of the land, blacks 13 per cent. There is one teacher for every 22 white children, but only one for every 60 blacks.

Archbishop Desmond Tutu

The Archbishop of Cape Town in South Africa, the Right Reverend Desmond Mpilo Tutu, is black. In 1984 he was awarded the Nobel Peace Prize, but in his own country, where he has no vote in parliamentary elections, of course, the government denounces him for meddling in politics. He has called upon other governments to impose trade sanctions on South Africa, while in his home land he tries to win justice for his own people without encouraging violence. He expressed his views in a sermon:

We are Christians not only in church on Sunday. Our Christianity is not something we put on, like our Sunday best, only for Sundays. It is for every day. We are Christians from Monday to Monday. We have no off day. We are Christians at play, at work, and at prayer. They are all rolled into one. It is not *either* worship *or* trying to do all the good works in our community. It is both. The wise men came to the child (Jesus) and worshipped. They gave him their gifts. We too must worship our God for ever and ever, and worship him by serving our neighbour today and tomorrow.

The doctrine which teaches that the black races of South Africa are the descendants of Ham is no longer officially held by any church, but apartheid remains. You will often find black and white Christians worshipping separately, but not everywhere. A past Prime Minister, Dr Malan, spoke of preserving 'the safety of the white race and of Christian civilisation', and that is what the South African government claims to be doing still, despite the fact that most blacks in South Africa are Christians. We have the strange position of the churches of the country denouncing a government which says it is Christian.

South Africa is the part of the world which everyone thinks of when racial discrimination is mentioned but it is an important issue wherever races live together. In 1988 a black, the Reverend Jesse Jackson, attempted to win the Democratic Party nomination to stand for election as the President of the USA. He was not successful and was not chosen as vice-presidential candidate either. Many said that if a black person were to stand he would fail automatically. America is not yet ready to elect a black president. In parts of the USA there is still discrimination in housing and work.

In the UK there have been examples of discrimination over the past 30 years. There are many reasons for the existence of so-called 'black churches', those where the congregation is of Afro-Caribbean origin. People with similar ways of worshipping and culture like to be together. However, one reason has been the lack of hospitality and welcome which some black Christians received when they first came to Britain and went to church.

Chapter	# Peace, War and Liberation Theology
19	

(see page 104)

PEACE AND WAR

A pacifist is someone who refuses to use violence and war as a means of settling disputes. It is not possible to tell whether the first Christians were pacificists or not. They were Jews and therefore exempt from the Roman army. Roman soldiers had to swear an oath of allegiance to the Roman emperor and worship him on special occasions, which the Jews as monotheists (see page 104) would not do. To have attempted to spread the Gospel by fighting was not a possibility even if they had wanted to – they were too small in numbers.

What happened when Christianity spread among Gentiles and soldiers became Christians is unclear. Perhaps they were able to buy themselves out of the army, their officers may have turned a blind eye to their refusal to worship the Emperor. What *is* known is that there were Christian soldiers in the army. In 172 CE the Emperor Marcus Aurelius was campaigning in the Danube region of Europe. His army was faced by drought and defeat. A rainstorm saved it from both. It is claimed that this was the result of the prayers of Christian solidiers in the regiment known as the *Legio XII Fulminata*, the Thundering Legion.

A clue to early Christian teaching to serving soldiers who became Christians may be contained in some advice given by John the Baptist, the preacher who paved the way for Jesus' ministry. He told them, 'No bullying; no blackmail; make do with your pay!' (Luke 3:14). Perhaps these words were remembered and written down because they gave helpful practical advice to soldier converts.

?

1   Dramatise a discussion between two Roman soldiers who witnessed the execution of St Alban (see page 22) and decided to become Christians. They are arguing about whether to stay in the army. One says 'yes', the other 'no'.
2   Write a letter home to Gaul from a Roman soldier to his parents, in which he explains his decision to become a Christian and leave the army (or stay in). Write a reply from his father, a veteran soldier.

When the temple guard came to arrest Jesus after the Last Supper, some of his followers drew their swords and one of them wounded the High Priest's servant, cutting off his right ear. Jesus ordered his friends to stop fighting, healed the wounded man and accepted arrest (Luke 22:49–53). In the story of Jesus' trial as told in John's Gospel, Jesus tells the Roman Governor, 'My kingdom does not belong to this world. If it did my followers would be fighting to save me from arrest by the Jews' (John 18:36).

The most famous words of Jesus on the use of outward force are found in the Sermon on the Mount. Here he says:

> 'You have learned that they were told, "An eye for an eye, and a tooth for a tooth." But what I tell you is this: Do not set yourself against the man who wrongs you. If someone slaps you on the right cheek, turn and offer him your left. If a man wants to sue you for your shirt, let him have your coat as well. If a man in authority makes you go one mile, go with him two.'
>
> Matthew 5:38–42

The Apostle Paul may have known these words, even though Matthew had not yet written his Gospel, when he wrote his letter to Christians in Rome. He quoted some words from the Jewish Bible, 'If your enemy is hungry, feed him; if he is thirsty, give him a drink; by doing this you will heap live coals on his head.' Then he added some words of his own, 'Do not let evil conquer you, but use good to defeat evil' (Romans 12:20–21). In that letter he then went on to advise Christians to obey the Roman state:

> Every person must submit to the supreme authorities. There is no authority but by act of God, and the existing authorities are instituted by him; consequently anyone who rebels against authority is resisting a divine institution, and those who so resist have themselves to thank for the punishment they will receive. For government, a terror to crime, has no terrors for good behaviour.
>
> Romans 13:1–3

In the First Letter of Peter there are similar words:

> Submit yourselves to every human institution for the sake of the Lord, whether to the sovereign as supreme, or to the governor as his deputy for the punishment of criminals and the commendation of those who do right. ... Give due honour to everyone: love to the brotherhood, reverence to God, honour to the sovereign.
>
> 1 Peter 2:13–17

Ironically, both Peter and Paul were probably executed in Rome by the supreme authority, the Emperor Nero. Did they change their views on obedience to the state as they were taken to the scaffold, one wonders!

The question did arise whether Christians should obey bad emperors, but for the most part it was felt that even they might be preferable to the anarchy which came with civil war and revolution. It seldom improved the lot of the oppressed poor.

In the Middle Ages a Christian scholar, Thomas Aquinas (*c.* 1225–74), considered most aspects of Christianity. Not surprisingly, for this was the time of the Crusades, he paid some attention to the Christian attitude to war. He laid down some conditions for a 'just war':

- it must be on the authority of the sovereign
- the cause must be just; the enemy must deserve to be attacked
- the intention of the belligerents must be rightful, that is, they must have good intentions and seek to establish peace and justice
- the good resulting from the war must outweigh the evil (for example, an attempt to free an oppressed group of people which resulted in their deaths as well as those of their enemies and many of their would-be rescuers could not be justified).

In the fourteenth century the Church added further conditions:

- war must be the last resort, used only when all other efforts had failed
- minimum necessary force should be used, with care being taken not to harm innocent noncombatants.

These conditions pose two problems: What is 'just'? and How do you protect innocent noncombatants? Most people in 1914 were told of the evils of German imperialism. Today many historians would be more inclined to see the causes in terms of economic and colonial expansion with little justification existing on either side. Both groups of nations engaged in the struggle claimed that *their* cause was 'just', that God was on their side and that the war was a kind of moral crusade. It is impossible to protect innocent noncombatants from the consequences of modern warfare, especially if nuclear of chemical weapons are used. Even in the Second World War, before the atomic bomb was dropped, thousands of children died in air raids on Britain and Germany.

All Christians would regard war as a last resort but only a minority of Christians are pacifist in the sense of being opposed to taking part in war under *any* circumstances. There are pacifists in almost every denomination but one group of Christians, the Quakers, is well-known for its observance of this principle. This is the Peace Testimony of the Society of Friends which is part of a Declaration presented to the English king Charles II as long ago as 1660:

> We utterly deny all outward wars and strife, and fighting with outward weapons, for any end, or under any pretence whatever; this is our testimony to the whole world. The Spirit of Christ by which we are guided is not changeable, so as once to command us from a thing as evil, and again to move into it; and we certainly know and testify to the world, that the spirit of Christ which leads us into all truth, will never move us to fight and war against any man with outward weapons, neither for the kingdom of Christ, nor for the kingdoms of the world.

Leaders of the larger churches may sometimes be seen blessing the launch of warships *but* they have tended to be outspoken against the use of nuclear weapons. The Second Vatican Council of the Roman Catholic Church (1962–5) said:

> Though the monstrous power of modern weapons acts as a deterrent, it is to be feared that the mere continuance of nuclear tests, undertaken with war in mind, will have fatal consequences for life on earth. Justice, right reason and humanity therefore, urgently demand that the arms race should cease; ... nuclear weapons should be banned.

> *Pacem in Terris*, Documents of Second Vatican Council, 1965

In 1982 the Anglican Church published a report entitled *The Church and the Bomb*. This urged Britain to get rid of its nuclear weapons. The report was debated in the General Synod, the governing body of the Church of England. Unilateral nuclear disarmament was rejected but there was agreement that nuclear weapons should only be used defensively and that Britain should not be first to use them.

Christians also seek to bring peace to areas of trouble in other ways. For example, in Northern Ireland there has been unrest since partition in 1922. The community tends to be divided along religious lines, with Protestants on the one side and Roman Catholics on the other; though anyone who has visited the province knows that this is an oversimplification. Also, there are many towns and villages in Northern Ireland where life continues peacefully. In 1965 a group of Catholics and Protestants decided to attempt to bring about reconciliation where there was hostility and suspicion. They have set up a community at Corrymeela where people of different backgrounds can come and live together for two days or up to a week, talk to one another, and attempt to understand one another. A week is not a long time, but it is a beginning, and for many of those who come the experience of talking with people they may have been taught to hate is new and challenging. There are also seed group meetings in which 20 men and women aged 18–21 come together every weekend for six months and then, hopefully, try to carry the lessons they have learned back into their communities.

?

Why do you think they are called 'seed group meetings'?

LIBERATION THEOLOGY

Liberation theology, which developed mainly in South America, is an attempt to wrestle with the way in which Christians should react to their *own* governments when they believe that they are oppressive, yet find that the normal methods of bringing about change in a democracy are denied them.

Since the time of the Emperor Constantine, church and state have frequently been in some kind of alliance. When missionaries converted a ruler to Christianity it was more likely than not that they would order their subjects to follow their example and mass baptisms would be organised. Throughout Europe, the major part of the Christian world in the Middle Ages, bishops combined the role of spiritual leader and civil servant. Most of them accepted the views of Paul and Peter that the civil authorities are appointed by God and should be obeyed, but sometimes conflicts of loyalty occurred.

In English history Thomas à Becket was murdered in his own cathedral of Canterbury because he had opposed Henry II. Henry VIII had the Bishop of Rochester, John Fisher, beheaded for refusing to support his wish to divorce Queen Catherine of Aragon and make himself supreme head of the church in England. Archbishop Lang played an important part in the discussions and events which resulted in the abdication of King Edward VIII in 1936. One of the reasons for the difficulties which Christians in Russia experienced after the Revolution of 1917 was that the Church had been an instrument of the Tsar, ruler of Russia. Since 1721, members of the Holy Synod, the body running church affairs in Russia, had been appointed by the Tsar. They were unlikely to oppose him, however much he ill treated the peasants.

Since the 1960s, Christians in South Africa, central and southern America, and Poland, as well as some other countries, have been outspoken against left- and right-wing governments, black- *or* white-dominated, which they believe ignore basic human rights and oppress the people. Roman Catholic clergy have often led the protest. In 1980 Archbishop Romero of El Salvador, a central American republic, was murdered by armed men who burst into a service while he was preaching, and shot him. He had criticised the government, though he had also said, 'If the church resorts to violence it will lose its authority to proclaim freedom in God's name.'

Archbishop Romero saying Mass in the cathedral in San Salvador.

Archbishop Romero *spoke* against the government. He did not join the armed struggle to overthrow it, as some priests and lay Christians have done.

Christians like Archbishop Tutu of South Africa or Nelson Mandela, the leader of the African National Congress who has spent more than 25 years in jail, are torn between resisting oppressive governments by non-violent means or recognising that the armed struggle against them may be justified.

 Find out more about Christians in South Africa and Latin America. Keep a scrapbook of any newspaper and magazine cuttings you find.

Christian Resistance to Hitler

Dietrich Bonhoeffer

One of the most famous men to face the non-violent dilemma was Dietrich Bonhoeffer, a German Lutheran, and theologian. He was one of the German Christians who opposed the Nazi regime of Hitler and was banned from preaching and teaching theology. He helped Jews to escape the death camps and used all legal means to oppose the government. Eventually, although it was against his principles of non-violence and obedience to the state, he concluded that the only way to rid his country of the Nazi government was to use force. He became involved in a bomb plot to assassinate Hitler, which failed, and was imprisoned. Hitler was determined that Bonhoeffer should not survive the defeat of Germany and had him executed not long before the Russians and Americans invaded Germany.

Another leader of protest against Hitler was Pastor Martin Niemoller, a hero of the First World War in which he had served as a U-boat (submarine) commander. He is reputed to have said:

> They came for the communists, but I kept silent because I was not a communist. They came for the Jews, but I kept silent because I was not a Jew. They came for the trade unionists, but I kept silent because I was not a trade unionist. Then they came for me, and there was no one left to speak for me.

These words are quoted in various forms and different people are given the credit of having spoken them first, but the words, and the lives of the two German Christians who were among the many who suffered for opposing Hitler, illustrate the problems which Christians face in deciding how to resist evil in the form of inhuman and unjust governments.

? Find out more about Christian resistance to Hitler from books, magazines and newspapers, especially about the work of Dietrich Bonhoeffer.

Christianity among the Religions

Do not read this chapter until you have read Chapter 17, Anti-Semitism, and Chapter 18, Racism and Apartheid.

We have already noted that Christianity began as a movement within Judaism and gradually emerged from it. The Apostles were both Jews and Christians. One of the last pieces of information that we have about St Paul is the story of his arrest which took place after a riot in the Jewish Temple. Paul, as an observant Jew, had gone there to fulfil purification rituals (Acts 21:25-9).

Just as Christians and Jews had drifted apart, so did Christians and Muslims at the time of the Crusades, though the Prophet Muhammad tried to establish good relationships, and in Spain, for example, Christian and Muslim scholars exchanged knowledge.

In the great period of European colonial expansion and mission (see page 25), it became usual for Christians to believe that theirs was the only true faith. After all Jesus had said, 'I am the way; the truth and I am the life; no one comes to the Father except by me' (John 14:6). The Apostle Peter had also said, in a speech about Jesus, 'There is no salvation in anyone else at all, for there is no other name under heaven, granted to men, by which we may receive salvation' (Acts 4:12).

Missionaries were often driven by a desire to save those who had not heard of Jesus from the fate which awaited them, eternal punishment in hell. One of the greatest of them, Francis Xavier (1506-52) who was later made a saint, had a Chinese servant who followed him devotedly through many difficulties and stood by him while others deserted him. However, he never became a Christian. When the servant suddenly died Xavier was sad to lose him, but said there was no point in praying for him. He was in hell beyond the help of prayers.

Not long ago a student who had visited a Hindu temple in England wrote in a report, 'What a great pity. They are such nice people and very religious, saying prayers, and singing hymns. But it is all a waste of time. They are not saying them through Jesus so God cannot listen to them.'

Christians do have a problem with the verses from John's Gospel and the Acts of the Apostles quoted above. Most could not regard them as propaganda statements made in the heat of debate. They cannot

In 1987 people of faith from many religions met and prayed together. Find out who the people in this photograph are.

believe that the words of John 14:6 were put into Jesus' mouth by the author. Some can. Some can also argue that the words did not refer to Jesus as a human being but as a manifestation of the divine nature, as the 'Word of God', as the writer of the Gospel describes him in chapter 1, 'the revelation of God'. Jesus, they might argue, was really saying that no one comes to God unless God calls him, or her.

There is the other kind of problem which lies behind Francis Xavier's actual remarks, 'We could not reward him for his goodness of heart, for he died without knowing God. We could never help him or pray for him even after his death, for he is in hell.'

This is the problem of whether the loving God which Christians believe in can really be so harsh. There may have been many reasons why Xavier's servant never became a Christian. He may have been obstinate. He may have believed that he already had a belief which seemed perfectly adequate. In the Acts of the Apostles the Holy Spirit changed people and converted them. Was it the servant's fault if the Holy Spirit did not transform him? Or was he actually a man of genuine faith but Xavier did not realise it because it did not come in the Christian form which he could recognise?

Christians today still find it hard to remain loyal to Jesus as God's last word, the saviour of humanity, the last and most perfect of God's many messengers (they often speak of the Finality of Christ), and yet find a place for the sincerely held beliefs of other people. The major denominations tend to say that God has revealed himself through the other religions of the world, as he did through Judaism. Here are some sentences from the Roman Catholic Second Vatican Council document, *Declaration on the Relationship of the Church to Non-Christian Religions:*

From ancient times down to the present, there has existed among diverse peoples a certain perception of that hidden power that hovers over the course of things and over the events of human life; at times, indeed, recognition can be found of a Supreme divinity and of a Supreme Father too. Such a perception and such a recognition instil the lives of these peoples with a profound religious sense. . . .

Thus, in Hinduism men contemplate the divine mystery and express it through an unspent fruitfulness of myths and through searching philosophical enquiry. They seek release from the anguish of our condition through ascetical practices or deep meditation or a loving, trusting flight towards God. . . .

Buddhism in its multiple forms acknowledges the radical insufficiency of this shifting world. It teaches a path by which men, in a confident spirit, can either reach a state of absolute freedom or attain supreme enlightenment by their own efforts or by higher assistance.

Upon Muslims, too, the Church looks with esteem. They adore one God, living and enduring, merciful and all-powerful, Maker of heaven and earth, and Speaker with men. . . .

The Church cannot forget that she received the revelation of the Old Testament through the people with whom God in his inexpressible mercy deigned to establish the Ancient Covenant. . . .

The Church repudiates all persecutions against any man. . . . she deplores the hatred, persecution, and displays of anti-Semitism directed against the Jews at any time and from any source. . . .

The Catholic Church rejects nothing which is true and holy in these religions. She looks with sincere respect upon those ways of conduct and of life, those rules and teachings which, though differing in many particulars from what she holds and sets forth, nevertheless often reflect a ray of that Truth which enlightens all men.

Documents of Second Vatican Council, 1965

Religions which are not specifically mentioned, such as Sikhism, had not attracted the attention of the theologians who framed the document, but they should be regarded as religions which 'reflect a ray of truth'.

Members of the traditions which are listed may not be satisfied with the attitude which the statement takes towards them. It might be said to suggest that they possess the truth, but not the whole truth. However, it does mark a change in the position of the Roman Catholic Church towards people of other faiths and is positive rather than negative. One wonders whether Hitler would have faced more opposition from Christians if these words had been written in 1935 instead of 1965.

1   If your school is in a multifaith district try to discover whether Christians and people of other faiths meet and work together.

2   Collect inter-faith statements made by other denominations. Compare them with one another and with the passages quoted above.

Chapter 21

The Future?

The story of Christianity continues to unfold. Its future is uncertain and unclear, but its members continue to put their trust in God as revealed in Jesus. It is risky to suggest which matters will concern Christians in the twenty-first century. You might like to make your own suggestions. Some may continue to be matters which outsiders may think to be unimportant, such as:

- relationships between one denomination and another
- whether women may become priests
- whether Roman Catholic priests should be allowed to marry.

Others may be:

- issues of leadership – Should there be a Pope or a head of the Anglican church who is not European and white?
- the sharing of the world's resources so that one fifth of the population (Europe and North America) no longer has about four-fifths of its wealth
- euthanasia – How will Christians respond to it when it becomes possible for people to have their lives prolonged almost without limit, but as little more than vegetables?
- conservation – So far men and women of science, governments and the average person 'in the street' have been rather leisurely in their approach to matters of survival, the green issues, but there are signs that a sense of urgency is developing.
- peace and war
- relations with other faiths.

Religions are likely to be thought worthy of consideration only if they can offer helpful guidance in personal and social areas of life which people regard as important. How Christians face the future could be one of the most interesting aspects of life in tomorrow's world.

Further Reading

Teachers' Books

W.M. Abbott, *The Documents of Vatican II* (Chapman, 1966)
D. Barton, *Discovering Chapel and Meeting Houses* (Shire Publications, 1975)
P. Bishop and M. Darton, *The Encyclopaedia of World Faiths* (Macdonald/Orbis, 1987)
D.M. Board, *A Way of Life: Being a Catholic Today* (Collins, 1982)
J.M. Bonino, *Revolutionary Theology Comes of Age* (SPCK, 1975)
J.D. Bosch, *Witness to the World: The Christian Mission in Theological Perspective* (Marshall, Morgan and Scott, 1980)
A. Brown (ed.), *Festivals in World Religions* (Longman, 1986)
W. Buhlmann, *The Coming of the Third Church: An Analysis of the Present and Future of the Church* (St Paul Publications, 1976)
H. Child and D. Colles, *Christians Symbols Ancient and Modern* (G. Bell, 1971)
F.L. Cross and E. Livingstone, *The Oxford Dictionary of the Christian Church* (OUP, 1974)
J.D. Douglas, *The New International Dictionary of the Christian Church* (Paternoster, 1974)
T. Downley (ed.), *The History of Christianity* (Lion, 1977)
A. Dunstan, *Interpreting Worship* (Mowbray, 1984)
M. Gilbert, *The Holocaust* (Collins, 1986)
J. Hinnells (ed.), *Handbook of Living Religions* (Penguin, 1984)
G.A. Lindbeck, *The Nature of Doctrine* (SPCK, 1984)
J. Macquarrie (ed.), *A Dictionary of Christian Ethics* (SCM, 1967)
P. Moore, *Christianity* (Ward Lock, 1982)
L. Ouspensky, *The Theology of the Icon* (St Vladimir's, New York, 1978)
R.R. Ruether, *Sexism and God Talk: Towards a Feminist Theology* (Simon and Schuster, 1983)
D. Sheppard, *The Black Experience in Britain* (Christian Action)
K. Ware, *The Orthodox Way* (Mowbray, 1979)
H.S. Wilson (ed.), *The Church on the Move* (Christian Literature Society, Madras, 1988)
Doctrine Commission of the Church of England, *Believing in the Church* (SPCK, 1981)

Pupils' Books

A. Brown, *The Christian World* (Macdonald, 1984) – a valuable introduction if it has not been used already
A. Burke, *The Dimensions of Christianity* (Kevin Mayhew, 1988) – a Roman Catholic perspective
D. Naylor and A. Smith, *Jesus: An Enquiry* (Macmillan, 1987)
S. Tompkins (ed.), *Meeting Religious Groups Series* (Lutterworth Press)
The Chichester Project series on Christianity (Lutterworth Press) covers most areas of Christian belief and practice. Full details from the Project Director: J.C. Rankin, 28 Worcester Road, Chichester, West Sussex.
The Christian Denominations series (Religious and Moral Education Press) covers most of the major denominations found in the UK.

Glossary

Anglican	A Christian who is a member of the Church of England or one of the Churches derived from it, e.g. Church of Australia.
apartheid	Apartness. Segregation of one group from another on grounds of gender, race, religion, or for other reasons.
apostle	One who is sent; used of the disciples of Jesus who were the first missionaries.
Apostles' Creed	Statement of Christian belief first used c. 390 CE, but linked by legend to the Apostles.
archbishop	A senior bishop, leader of the Church in a particular country or region.
Ascension	The return of Jesus to heaven to assume full divine authority.
Baptist	A Christian denomination (or member of it), which believes in believers' baptism by total immersion.
bishop	The highest order of clergy in the Roman Catholic, Orthodox and Anglican Churches, regarded as successors of the Apostles.
charismatic	A person who possesses such gifts of the Holy Spirit as the ability to heal or speak in tongues.
Church	(1) The collective term for the Christian community worldwide. Also (2) used of a particular denomination, e.g. Church of Scotland.
church	(1) Building in which Christians worship, or (2) Christians who meet there.
clergy	Ordained ministers; spiritual leaders of the Church.
council	An assembly of bishops.
disciple	One who accepts the teachings of another.
doctrine	An approved teaching of the Church.
ecumenical	Literally one world; used of the attempts to unify the Church.
elder	A lay person appointed to help in the administration of a church.
elements	The bread and wine used at the Eucharist, Mass or Communion service.
faith	May mean 'trust', as 'I have faith in you', or belief, 'the Christian faith'.
Gentile	Originally meant peoples, races or nations, but in the New Testament and now it means non-Jew.
gospel	'Good news', i.e. the message of salvation through faith in Jesus.
Gospel	One of the four New Testament books in which the good news (gospel) is contained. They are records of the good news, not biographies.
heaven	Abode of God and his angels; destiny of the faithful; a state of eternal bliss.
hell	The abode of those who reject God; not a place but a state of being.
heretic	Someone who holds a belief contrary to the doctrine of a religion.
holy	Set aside from ordinary use to be used only in the service of God, or belonging to God (e.g. Holy Bible).
laity	Literally 'people'; members of a denomination who are not ordained (the clergy).
Last Supper	The last meal which Jesus ate with his disciples, on the night of his arrest.
Messiah	Literally the anointed one, the expected deliverer of the Jews.
miracle	A sign of divine power.
Nicene Creed	Statement of Christian belief agreed at the Council of Nicea in 325 CE.
parable	A method of teaching through story-telling.
Passover	A Jewish festival celebrating deliverance of the Jews from slavery in Egypt.
patriarch	(1) One of the early leaders of Israel up to the time of Jacob. (2) The bishops of Rome, Alexandria, Antioch, Constantinople, or Jerusalem.
Pope	Literally, father; the bishop of Rome and leader of Roman Catholics.
prayer	Personal or corporate spiritual communion with God usually in the form of words, involving listening as well as speaking.
sacrament	A rite of the Church which is a sign of spiritual blessing or grace.
Talmud	Literally 'study'; the collected content and discussions of the oral Jewish Torah.
Ten Commandments	The most famous of the 613 instructions contained in the Torah. Found in the Bible in Exodus 19–20 and Deuteronomy 5.
Torah	The first five books of the Jewish Bible, the Christian Old Testament.
yoga	Literally 'yoke'; meditation and self-control, to achieve spiritual liberation.

Index